W9-APS-543

Key Concepts 1

- Listening, Note Taking, and
- Speaking Across the Disciplines

Key Concepts 1

- **Listening, Note Taking, and**
- **Speaking Across the Disciplines**

Elena Vestri Solomon

Hillsborough Community College

John L. Shelley

 Additional information and activities can be found at the *Key Concepts 1* website: *elt.heinle.com/keyconcepts*.

 HEINLE
CENGAGE Learning™

Australia • Brazil • Japan • Korea • Mexico • Singapore • Spain • United Kingdom • United States

Key Concepts 1: Listening, Note Taking, and Speaking Across the Disciplines
Elena Vestri Solomon / John L. Shelley

Publisher: Patricia A. Coryell

Senior Development Editor: Kathy Sands-Boehmer

Development Editor: Kathleen M. Smith

Editorial Assistant: Evangeline Bermas

Project Editor: Kerry Doyle

Executive Marketing Manager: Annamarie Rice

Marketing Assistant: Andrew Whitacre

Compositor: Publishing Services

Cover Image: © David Zaitz/Photonica

© 2006 Heinle, Cengage Learning

ALL RIGHTS RESERVED. No part of this work covered by the copyright herein may be reproduced, transmitted, stored or used in any form or by any means graphic, electronic, or mechanical, including but not limited to photocopying, recording, scanning, digitizing, taping, Web distribution, information networks, or information storage and retrieval systems, except as permitted under Section 107 or 108 of the 1976 United States Copyright Act, without the prior written permission of the publisher.

For permission to use material from this text or product, submit all requests online at **cengage.com/permissions** Further permissions questions can be emailed to **permissionrequest@cengage.com**

Library of Congress Number: 2005929071

ISBN-13: 978-0-618-38240-8

ISBN-10: 0-618-38240-2

Heinle
25 Thomson Place
Boston, MA 02210
USA

Cengage Learning is a leading provider of customized learning solutions with office locations around the globe, including Singapore, the United Kingdom, Australia, Mexico, Brazil and Japan. Locate our local office at: **international.cengage.com/region**

Cengage Learning products are represented in Canada by Nelson Education, Ltd.

Visit Heinle online at **elt.heinle.com**
Visit our corporate website at **cengage.com**

Photo Credits: Page 1 © John Henley Photography/CORBIS; Page 21 © Images.com/CORBIS; Page 39 © Brand X/SuperStock; Page 61 Reprinted with permission. Architect of the Capitol, Collection of the U.S. House of Representatives; Page 70 © Bettmann/CORBIS; Page 81 © R. Morley/PhotoLink/Getty Images; Page 85 © Hulton-Deutsch Collection/CORBIS; Page 105 © Leo Meyer/Painet Inc.

Printed in the United States of America
7 8 9 10   12 11

Contents

Additional information and activities can be found at the
Key Concepts 1 website: *elt.heinle.com/keyconcepts.*

Key Concepts 1 Skills Overview

	Listening for ...			**Speaking**
Chapter	**Strategy/ Pronunciation**	**Note Taking**	**Discourse Markers**	
1	context	• observe • record • review	overview of functions	interviewing
2	pronunciation differences in *the*	outlining	various functions	conducting surveys
3	distinguishing regular past tense and past participles	word maps	sequencing	extemporaneous speaking
4	• phrasal verbs • reduced ə sounds	Cornell method	transition signals	debate
5	• phrasal verbs • word combinations in sound groups	key word method	more transition signals	group presentation
6	• phrasal verbs • reduction strings	paragraph method	introducing new subjects and ideas	researching and summarizing topics

Introduction

Key Concepts 1 is the first in a two-volume series focusing on the academic skills of listening, note taking, speaking, and vocabulary building. The most important element of the *Key Concepts* series is the subject matter itself, both in the text and on the accompanying audio program. The text revolves around the academic disciplines. Each chapter covers a topic from one of the following: college success, social science, business, history, biological science, and humanities. Mirroring general education requirements found in most community colleges and universities, *Key Concepts* allows students to refine their academic skills through the understanding of the main concepts and lecture points they will encounter in higher education.

The theme of each chapter is the driving force behind the listening skills exercises, which involve understanding dialogue, discrete listening and pronunciation, and classroom note taking. The group work and speaking activities also focus on the theme of each chapter, offering the student a consistent and unified approach to learning the material. Because the texts are aimed at students in the mid- and high-intermediate levels, the listening activities—particularly the lectures—are designed to allow for $I + 1$ input as well. In addition to content-specific vocabulary, each chapter of *Key Concepts* introduces students to twenty vocabulary items from the Academic Word List and offers extensive practice with these lexical items. The Academic Word List, developed by Averil Coxhead, is a compilation of the most frequently found vocabulary items in college-level arts, commerce, law, and science texts. See more about the Academic Word List under Contents of a Chapter below.

For many ESL students, the term "academic English" brings to mind grammar, writing, and reading skills, and too few listening/speaking texts focus on improving academic *oral* communication. By contrast, *Key Concepts* prepares students for the many academic tasks they will face in higher education by providing an active listening/speaking component contextualized to the academic material—understanding key points of the disciplines, discrete listening, note-taking strategies, understanding discourse markers, academic vocabulary practice—as well as speaking strategies.

Text Organization

The skills practiced in *Key Concepts* can be broken down into the following:

- 50% listening: main ideas, details, inference, note taking

- 25% vocabulary building: high-frequency vocabulary, content-based vocabulary, discourse markers (transitions)

- 25% speaking: recycling vocabulary and content, negotiating meaning, formal presentation skills, group problem solving

The text is divided into six chapters and seven appendixes. Mirroring current trends and best practices in higher education, Chapter 1 introduces students to the "freshman experience" with a primer on academic study and college success skills. Chapters 2 through 6 each focus on one particular field of the major college disciplines. The appendixes include Academic Word List entries, speaking tips and sample speaking evaluation forms, discourse markers by function, common phrasal verbs, and note-taking strategies and symbols.

Contents of a Chapter

Listening 1: Short Conversations

The first listening task includes the following activities: Getting Ready to Listen with **brainstorming and discussion**, **listening** for meaning and inference, and **responding** to the conversations.

Listening 2: Mini-Lecture

To prepare for the second listening task, students are introduced to **vocabulary** items from the Academic Word List. Students then practice the vocabulary through different exercise formats. A new **note-taking strategy** is presented in every chapter, and students are asked to practice the note-taking method while listening to the mini-lecture. **Comprehension questions** follow after the students have reviewed their notes.

Academic Word List Practice

The Academic Word List figures prominently in the *Key Concepts* series. *Key Concepts 1* contains the first 120 lexical items on the list. These are the **most frequently used vocabulary words** in college-level texts. Each chapter includes definitions of the key words and various vocabulary exercises, allowing for student practice of the key terms. In addition, the Standard American Heritage phonetic spelling of each word is provided in the chapters and in Appendix 1.

Listening 3: Listening Strategy

This **discrete listening** activity exploits a variety of points in the short conversations, the mini-lectures, or the extended lectures and asks students to concentrate on specific **pronunciation** elements or **vocabulary** items.

Listening 4: Extended Lecture

To prepare students for the extended lecture portion of the chapter, **discourse marker exercises** are included. Students practice the **meaning and usage** of specific discourse markers to better prepare them for the use of these markers in the extended lecture. Additional **vocabulary** from the Academic Word List is presented in this section. **Note taking** is reinforced as students practice the note-taking strategy of the chapter. **Comprehension questions** and a **critical thinking** activity follow.

Speaking

Each chapter ends with students practicing different speaking activities. They include interviewing, developing surveys in groups, extemporaneous speaking, debating, presenting as a group, and summarizing.

Each chapter includes additional activity ideas related to the chapter theme. Time permitting, instructors may choose to have all the students participate in this expansion activity or assign it as an extra credit activity.

Online Resources

Additional Web Activities for Students at elt.heinle.com/keyconcepts

The *Key Concepts* series also offers additional activities using audio recordings. These listening activities are connected to the disciplines presented in each chapter. Students can listen to the lecture, then practice note taking, listening, and vocabulary by logging on to the Heinle website at *elt.heinle.com/keyconcepts*.

Instructor Manual and Answer Key

The instructor manual and answer key for the *Key Concepts* series are available on the Heinle website at *elt.heinle.com/keyconcepts*.

Assessment

Every chapter contains additional mini-lectures that are available online for instructors to use as assessment tools. Comprehensive tests accompany the lectures. These tests include areas for students to take notes, comprehension questions, and vocabulary items from the Academic Word List. Instructors may use the audio programs or choose to deliver the lectures themselves. For these instructors, note cards can be downloaded, printed, and used to present the lecture "naturally" to the class. Comprehension tests can be downloaded by instructors and given to students. The instructor site also contains a variety of web activities for instructors to give to students.

Acknowledgments

We would like to thank the many faculty members of Hillsborough Community College who gave tireless input and feedback on the academic requirements of their disciplines. Their expertise was paramount to the creation of the content-driven chapters. We express equal gratitude to our ESL colleagues who shared their ideas and insights on the value of oral communication and methods of achieving academic success in listening and speaking.

Our editors, Susan Maguire and Kathy Sands-Boehmer, gave us guidance and support throughout the entire process, for which we are extremely grateful. We couldn't have asked for a better development editor, Kathleen Smith, whose ideas, feedback, and input have made our work that much better. Of course, this series would have never been possible without the constant guidance and support of Keith S. Folse, friend and mentor.

Our gratitude also goes out to the many reviewers who commented on our manuscripts, offering advice and suggestions that helped create our final product. They are:

Carol Auerbach, *Northern Virginia Community College*

Michael Berman, *Montgomery College*

Keri Bjorklund, *Laramie Community College*

Gwendolyn Charvis, *North Harris College*

Cynthia Dunham-Gonzalez, *Seminole Community College*

Kathy Flynn, *Glendale Community College*

Beverly Gandall, *Santa Ana College*

Elizabeth Gilfillan, *Houston Community College*

Margo Harder, *South Seattle Community College*

Michael Khirallah, *Oakland Community College*

Shirley Terrell, *Collin County Community College*

Last, our thanks go out to our many ESL and EFL students, who, over the years, have given us the drive to continue to learn, evaluate, and better ourselves as educators and individuals.

Elena Vestri Solomon
John L. Shelley

1 The Student Experience: Success in College

CSC 121
College Success (3)
This interdisciplinary course helps students develop skills that are necessary for a successful college experience. The course focuses on academic support for students, with topics including goal assessment, time management, critical thinking, note- and test-taking skills, and communication practice. Guest speakers appear regularly in this class.

Making the decision to go to college is not as tough as it was in the past. Most people are aware that an advanced education can open many career doors that a high school diploma cannot. Once you decide to go to college, there are many issues to consider.

Here are some of the questions students have about college study:

Should I choose a community college or a university?

Once I choose a school, how do I choose a major?

What will my teachers expect of me?

What skills do I need to be successful in college?

This chapter will help you understand some **key concepts** of success in college, such as

- understanding the differences between colleges and universities
- making smart choices
- developing note-taking skills

You will also learn and practice some academic skills for success.

Get Ready to Listen

ACTIVITY ❶ *Brainstorming and Discussion*

Working with a partner, list as much information as you can about the topics in the boxes below. Don't worry about correct spelling or writing complete sentences. When you have finished, share your answers with your teacher and classmates.

Community Colleges	Universities

Successful College Students

Responding to Questions and Giving Advice

Commonly Used Modals for Giving Advice

Suggestions
can
could
might

Advice
should
ought to
had better

Obligation/Necessity
must
have to

Positive verbal interaction with other students and with teachers is one strategy for being a successful student. Maintaining respectful relationships is very important and can be beneficial to everyone involved. When you talk to people, especially people you don't know well, it is important to answer questions and make suggestions politely.

The phrases below are commonly used when responding to a question or giving advice to help solve a problem.

Phrases Followed by a Simple Verb	Phrases Followed by a Gerund (verb + *-ing*) or a Noun/Pronoun
Why don't you …?	How about …?
Why not …?	What about …?
What if you …?	Try …
You might want to …	Have you ever thought of …?
You could always …	
Maybe you could …	
You'd better …	
If I were you, I would …	
You should …	
Shouldn't you …?	

Listen and Respond

ACTIVITY 2

Listen to Conversations

Listen to the short conversations. Fill in the blanks with the words you hear.

1. A: I don't know where to go to college! I need help!

   B: Have you ever _____ talking to the school counselor?

2. A: I got a 53 on the vocabulary quiz!

   B: You _____ want to study harder next time.

3. A: I'm tired of driving around looking for a parking space on campus.

   B: You _____ always check out the bus schedule.

4. A: Tuition's going to be raised again next year.

   B: Then we _____ look into getting a loan or a grant.

5. A: I can't read any of my notes.

   B: _____ skipping lines in your notebook next time.

6. A: Dr. Sherman, can you tell us what's going to be on the final exam?

   B: If _____ you, I'd review all the main points from Chapters 1 through 8.

7. A: The books at the bookstore are way too expensive.

   B: _____ going to the used bookstore downtown?

8. A: All the Freshman English classes are closed already. We can't sign up!

   B: _____ we _____ take English online.

Give Advice

You are having some problems in class. A friend tries to help you by making some suggestions. For each problem situation below, list some possible solutions. Use the phrases and modals on page 3. Share your suggestions with a partner.

1. You're not sure what courses to take.

   Suggestions: _Why don't you talk to a counselor?_ _____

   _____

   _____

2. You keep coming to class late.

   Suggestions: _____

   _____

   _____

3. You recently failed an exam.

   Suggestions: _____

   _____

   _____

4. Your classmates talk too much during class.

   Suggestions: _____

   _____

   _____

5. You didn't understand something that the teacher just explained.

   Suggestions: _____

   _____

   _____

6. You missed a class and don't have the class notes.

   Suggestions: _____

   _____

   _____

7. You have scheduled a doctor's appointment for the same time as an exam.

   Suggestions: _____

   _____

   _____

8. You need to increase your vocabulary skills.

   Suggestions: _____

   _____

   _____

9. You lost your textbook.

   Suggestions: _____

   _____

10. You didn't have time to study, so you are not prepared for tomorrow's test.

   Suggestions: _____

   _____

Compare your answers with your classmates. As a group, choose the five best or most interesting suggestions made for each problem. Share them with the class.

LISTENING 2 ● **Mini-Lecture: Community Colleges vs. Universities**

Vocabulary

In *Key Concepts 1*, you will practice many vocabulary words from the Academic Word List, which contains the most frequently used vocabulary words found in college-level textbooks. You may be familiar with some of the vocabulary words. Although the definitions are important, it is also helpful to look at the pronunciation of each word, found in brackets ([ ]) before the definitions. Try reading the word aloud using this phonetic spelling.

NOTE: For a complete list of the Academic Word List vocabulary in *Key Concepts 1*, see Appendix 1, page 125. Appendix 1 also includes the standard *American Heritage Dictionary* phonetic spellings in the list below.

Academic Word List

Practice reading and saying aloud these vocabulary words. How many of the words do you already know?

(word) (how to pronounce it) (part of speech (noun)) (verb)

1. **credit** [krĕd´ ĭt] n. belief or confidence; trust; approval or praise for some act or quality; a unit of study. v. to trust or believe in; to regard somebody as having done something good

   Diane didn't get the <u>credit</u> for writing up the company's budget, so she's very angry right now. (n)
   Full-time college students usually take between twelve and fifteen <u>credits</u>. (n)
   I <u>credit</u> my parents for helping me be successful in college. (v)

2. **distinct** [dĭ stĭngkt´] adj. different; separate

   There is a <u>distinct</u> personality difference between my twin brothers.

3. **evaluate** [ĭ val´ yōō āt´] v. to find out or estimate the value of something; examine and appraise

   At the end of the semester, we're going to <u>evaluate</u> our professor's course.

---

4. **final** [fī´ nəl] adj. occurring at the end; last

   The <u>final</u> exam has been rescheduled to next week.

5. **proceed** [prə cēd´] v. to move forward or onward; continue

   If we <u>proceed</u> for ten more miles, we'll reach the Canadian border.

6. **require** [rĭ kwīr´] v. to be in need of

   My new car <u>requires</u> a lot of professional maintenance.

7. **respond** [rĭ spŏnd´] v. to make a reply; answer

   I was so nervous that I couldn't <u>respond</u> to the teacher's question.

8. **select** [sĭ lĕkt´] v. to choose; pick out. adj. carefully chosen; of special quality

   We haven't had time to <u>select</u> a class president yet. (v)
   We chose a <u>select</u> location for our wedding reception. (adj)

9. **specific** [spĭ sĭf´ ĭk] adj. stated clearly and in detail; special, distinctive, or unique. n. (pl.) particulars; details

   I don't know the <u>specific</u> location of next week's party. (adj)
   The <u>specifics</u> of the final exam haven't been announced yet. (n)

10. **transfer** [trăns fûr´] or [trăns´ fər] v. to move or cause something to pass from one place, person, or thing to another; n. the moving of something or someone from one place, person, or thing to another

    My community college credits <u>transferred</u> easily to the university. (v)
    The accountant requested a <u>transfer</u> to another division. (n)

 ACTIVITY 4 | *Vocabulary Practice*

Each numbered sentence contains an underlined word from the Academic Word List. Read each sentence, then circle the letter of the sentence that has the same meaning as the original.

1. Joe wants to <u>transfer</u> to another class.
   a. He wants to drop out of his classes.
   b. He wants to move to another class.
   c. He wants to add another class.

2. Dr. Sherman <u>selected</u> the information for the midterm exam.
   a. She changed the information for the midterm exam.
   b. She moved the information for the midterm exam.
   c. She chose the information for the midterm exam.

3. Our teacher Ms. Yost will <u>evaluate</u> us next week.
   a. She will examine and appraise our work.
   b. She will lower our grades next week.
   c. She will give us time to do research next week.

4. College algebra is <u>required</u> before taking calculus.
   a. It is a good idea to take college algebra before taking calculus.
   b. You must take college algebra before taking calculus.
   c. It is not necessary to take college algebra before taking calculus.

5. Sam couldn't <u>respond</u> to the professor's question.
   a. He couldn't understand the question.
   b. He couldn't answer the question.
   c. He couldn't hear the question.

6. "Can we <u>proceed</u> to the next point?"
   a. "Can we analyze this?"
   b. "Can we stop?"
   c. "Can we move on to something else?"

7. He has a <u>specific</u> plan to improve his quiz grades.
   a. He is not sure of his plan to improve his quiz grades.
   b. He has a definite plan to improve his quiz grades.
   c. He has changed his plan to improve his quiz grades.

8. Henry didn't get enough <u>credit</u> for the research paper he wrote.
   a. His teacher did not praise him enough on his research paper.
   b. His teacher did not receive the research paper.
   c. His teacher did not like the way Henry wrote his research paper.

9. My <u>final</u> grade in philosophy was incredible.
   a. My first philosophy grade was excellent.
   b. I don't know my philosophy grade.
   c. I will not have any more philosophy grades.

10. The syllabus for Freshman English has <u>distinct</u> objectives.
    a. The objectives are confusing.
    b. There are many separate objectives on the syllabus.
    c. The objectives are clear.

Taking Notes

Good note taking involves much more than following and understanding what the speaker is saying and writing it down. There are three important steps that students should follow in order to understand a lecture fully.

1. **Observe.** Pay full attention to the statements made by the teacher.

2. **Record.** Write down the information (take notes.)

3. **Review.** Look through your notes afterwards—adding, eliminating, or changing some information. This will help you prepare for the next day's information.

Each step of this process depends on the others. Study this diagram.

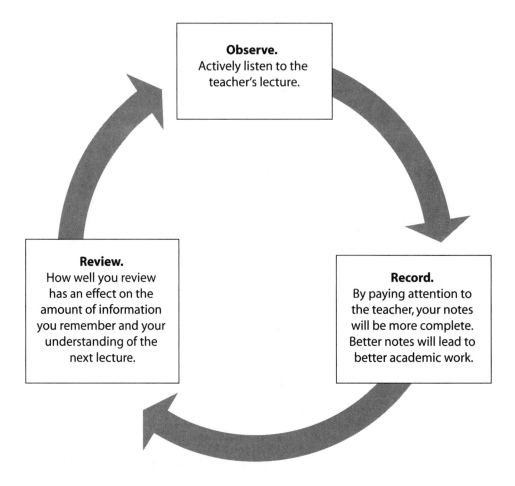

Observe.
Actively listen to the teacher's lecture.

Record.
By paying attention to the teacher, your notes will be more complete. Better notes will lead to better academic work.

Review.
How well you review has an effect on the amount of information you remember and your understanding of the next lecture.

NOTE: For more information about note-taking strategies, see Appendix 5, page 139.

Discourse Markers

What Is a Discourse Marker?

Discourse markers are words or phrases that help listeners (and readers) understand the flow of information. These words and phrases signal important pieces of information. They help us to understand and, more important, predict what will come next. We often use discourse markers when we speak. For instance, when you explain to your friends why you like a certain movie, you probably use discourse markers to add information.

> I liked *Terminator 3* because of the great special effects. I enjoyed the acting **as well.**

The phrase *as well* can be considered a discourse marker because it marks additional information—in this case, the acting.

In your study of English, you may have encountered *transition words*. Writers use transition words to achieve cohesion with phrases that introduce (*to begin*), give examples (*for example,*), and conclude (*in conclusion*). In speaking, discourse markers function much like transition words.

NOTE: For a more complete list of discourse markers, see Appendix 6, page 140.

Determine What's Important

When teachers give lectures, they provide a lot of information. However, not all of the information they present is related to the content of the course. It's helpful to learn how to understand discourse markers to determine what information relates to the topic of the lecture.

Example 1

The teacher states, "**I want to stress** that Martin Luther King Jr. was not alone in his struggle for civil rights."

CONTENT: "Martin Luther King Jr. was not alone in his struggle for civil rights" tells us that Martin Luther King Jr. and other people involved in civil rights are the subjects of the lecture.

DISCOURSE MARKER: "I want to stress" marks a certain characteristic of the information.

discourse marker showing emphasis → "**I want to stress** that Martin Luther King Jr. was not alone in his struggle for civil rights."

content

In this example, the phrase **I want to stress** is a discourse marker that shows *emphasis*. The teacher believes that the information following this discourse marker is of particular importance.

Example 2

Let's imagine that the same teacher uses a different discourse marker with the same content.

discourse marker showing contrast → "**On the other hand**, Martin Luther King Jr. was not alone in his struggle for civil rights."

content

In this example, the discourse marker **on the other hand** gives *contrasting* information. The teacher is giving a cue that the information coming up is in contrast to the previous information.

Question for You

Read the following sentence. Which of the two phrases following the underlined discourse marker sounds logical? To check your answer, go to page 19.

"John F. Kennedy was assassinated. <u>On the other hand</u>, (Gandhi was shot./Winston Churchill died of a stroke.)"

The better your knowledge of discourse markers, the better you will understand a teacher's lectures. Here is a list of discourse markers you will hear in this unit.

List of Discourse Markers	
Function	**Discourse Marker**
Introducing new information	Today we are going to consider
Giving background information	It goes without saying
Defining	*X* is actually
Listing	First,
Showing a connection	Pertaining to
Emphasizing	I want to stress
Clarifying	What I mean to say is
Shifting subtopics	Now, I'd like to turn to
Giving further information	Furthermore,
Giving contrasting information	On the other hand,
Digressing	By the way,

NOTE: For a complete list of discourse markers, see Appendix 6, page 140.

Listen and Respond

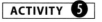

Listen and Use Strategies You Learned

First Listening: Listen for Discourse Markers You will hear a lecture played two times. Try to get used to the speaker's voice and tone. Listen specifically for discourse markers. Only six of the following discourse markers appear in this lecture; put a check mark next to the ones that you hear.

_____ Today we are going to consider   _____ Pertaining to

_____ It goes without saying   _____ On the other hand,

_____ By the way,   _____ For instance,

_____ What I mean to say is   _____ Now, I'd like to turn to

_____ I want to stress   _____ Furthermore,

_____ First,   _____ *X* is actually

Second Listening: Listen and Take Notes Listen to the mini-lecture again and take notes on the content in the space below. In later chapters, you will practice some specific note-taking styles. For now, use whatever style of note taking is most comfortable for you. Don't worry about correct spelling or complete sentences.

Remember that the content of a lecture is very important and will most likely appear on a test. For this reason, good note takers focus on key content words and ideas rather than writing down every word. This lecture also features the Academic Word List vocabulary from pages 5–6.

NOTE: If you use symbols instead of words to save time while taking notes, refer to Appendix 4 on pp. 136–137 for more information on using note-taking symbols.

Answer Questions about the Mini-Lecture

Read the following statements about the mini-lecture. Circle the letter of the one statement in each group that is true. Refer to your notes from Activity 5 to help you.

1. a. A high school diploma is necessary before going to a community college or university.
   b. A high school diploma is suggested before going to a community college or university.
   c. A high school diploma is not required to go to a community college or university.
   d. A student must proceed to a community college or university after receiving a high school diploma.

2. a. Three general types of courses are offered at community colleges and universities.
   b. Four general types of courses are offered at community colleges and universities.
   c. Two general types of courses are offered at community colleges and universities.
   d. One basic type of course is offered at community colleges and universities.

3. a. One of the courses mentioned in the lecture is physical studies.
   b. One of the courses mentioned in the lecture is social science.
   c. One of the courses mentioned in the lecture is social studies.
   d. One of the courses mentioned in the lecture is mathematical science.

4. a. Each course generally equals 34 hours.
   b. Each course is generally between 30 and 40 hours long.
   c. Each course is generally between 3 and 4 hours long.
   d. Each course can be from 3 to 40 hours long.

5. a. An AA degree is given after one year of study.
   b. An AA degree is given after a few years of study.
   c. An AA degree is given after three years of study.
   d. An AA degree is given after two years of study.

6. a. Many students decide to enter a university after getting their AA or AS degree.
   b. Many students decide to get a job after getting their AA or AS degree.
   c. Many students decide to transfer to another AA or AS program after finishing community college.
   d. Many students earn an AA degree after they graduate from a university.

7. a. Most students who graduate from a four-year college do not look for work.
   b. Most students who graduate from a four-year college with a bachelor's degree begin to look for jobs.
   c. Most students who graduate from a four-year college decide to continue their education.
   d. Most students who graduate from a four-year college receive a degree in advertising.

8. a. Companies prefer to hire graduates with an associate's degree rather than those with a bachelor's degree.
   b. The job market is approximately the same for students with an associate's degree or a bachelor's degree.
   c. Companies prefer to hire graduates with a four-year degree.
   d. Students with AA degrees will never get jobs.

Now compare answers with a classmate. If your answers are different, look at each other's notes to find the specific areas where they differ.

LISTENING 3 ● **Listening Strategy: Listen for Context**

Listen for Context

If you don't know the meaning of a word, you can sometimes figure out part or all of its meaning if you understand the words around it—its *context*. Try to guess the meaning of a word you hear by looking at its connection to other words. You can use this strategy when reading new information, but it is also useful in improving your listening skills. Listening carefully to the context, as well as to the content and the tone, can help you better understand the meaning of a word, or at least its connotation.

ACTIVITY **7**

Guess Meaning from Context

As you listen to the sentences, try to figure out the meaning of the *italicized* word in each item. Circle the correct letter.

1. The word *previous* has something to do with:
   a. time   b. quality   c. quantity

2. The word *section* is related to:
   a. students   b. location   c. religion

3. The word *maintain* is related to:
   a. stopping something   b. understanding something
   c. continuing something

4. *Surveying* class notes means:
   a. reviewing the notes   b. destroying the notes
   c. understanding the notes

5. A *journal* is something:
   a. written   b. mental   c. verbal

6. A *chapter* is something:
   a. spoken   b. heard   c. written

7. A *text* is something:
   a. shared   b. abstract   c. concrete

8. An *approach* is
   a. universal (the same for everybody)
   b. unique (different for different people)
   c. unimportant

9. The word *items* is related to
   a. things in a list   b. personal ideas   c. mental pictures

10. A *context* is:
    a. uncommon   b. permanent   c. changeable

LISTENING 4 ● Extended Lecture: About Note Taking

 ACTIVITY 8   *Check the Definitions*

The definitions of the words from Activity 7 are listed below. You will hear these words in the extended lecture. Read the definitions, then go back to Activity 7 and review your answers. Are there any answers that you want to change?

Vocabulary

Academic Word List

Practice reading and saying aloud these vocabulary words. How many do you already know?

1. **approach** [ə prōch´] n. a way or method of dealing or working with somebody or something. v. to come near

   My professor likes to use a visual approach when she lectures to us. (n)
   The student approached the teacher after the lecture to ask a few questions. (v)

2. **chapter** [chăp´ tər] n. a main division of a book

   Our writing book is divided into ten chapters, each for a different rhetorical style.

3. **context** [kŏn´ tĕkst] n. The part of a statement or text that surrounds a particular word or passage and makes its meaning clear

   Many words mean different things depending on the context of the conversation.

4. **item** [ī´ təm] n. a single thing or unit

   The vocabulary list contains thirty items.

5. **journal** [jûr´ nəl] n. a daily record of events; a diary or log

   Every night before going to bed, Joanna writes a few notes in her journal.

6. **maintain** [mān tān´] v. to continue something

   After Susan lost her job, she had to sell some of her jewelry in order to maintain her lifestyle.

7. **previous** [prē´ vē əs] adj. existing or happening before something else

   Our previous quiz was much harder than today's quiz.

8. **section** [sĕk´ shən] n. one of several parts that make up something; a piece

   The SAT is separated into three sections.

9. **survey** [sûr´ vā´] n. a detailed study of a group's opinions or behavior. [sər vā´] or [sûr´ vā´] v. to look over the parts or features of something

The phone company sent out a ten-question <u>survey</u> to see if its customers would be interested in additional telephone services. (n)

I <u>surveyed</u> my notes after the lecture. (v)

10. **text** [tĕkst] n. the main part of a written work

You can't answer the questions unless you look at the <u>text</u>.

ACTIVITY 9   *Vocabulary Practice*

Circle the letter of the word that best completes each sentence.

1. My _____ teacher didn't explain math very well, which is why I don't understand it now.
   a. context   b. item   c. previous   d. approach

2. At first I thought my lab partner was mad at me, but in the _____ of the conversation, I realized that he wasn't.
   a. chapter   b. context   c. maintain   d. item

3. In order to _____ his grade point average, Joey spends almost every night at the library studying.
   a. maintain   b. approach   c. survey   d. section

4. Everyone has a specific _____ to studying before a test. Some people write things down again and again.
   a. survey   b. chapter   c. approach   d. section

5. This text is separated into three _____: listening, note taking, and speaking.
   a. approaches   b. sections   c. contexts   d. surveys

6. The admissions advisor asked us to fill out a twenty-question _____ about our academic interests.
   a. survey   b. item   c. context   d. journal

7. The literature book was so large that the class could get through only five of the twenty _____.
   a. journals   b. items   c. chapters   d. approaches

8. The university library will let you check out a maximum of ten _____.
   a. items   b. surveys   c. chapters   d. contexts

9. The reading test had two sections: a vocabulary section with forty questions and a reading section with three _____ to read and answer questions about.
   a. approaches   b. texts   c. contexts   d. sections

10. Our writing teacher Ms. Saad asked us to keep a _____ to jot down our personal thoughts.
    a. journal   b. context   c. text   d. survey

Listen and Respond

Listen and Use Strategies You Learned

First Listening: Listen for Discourse Markers The extended lecture about successful note-taking strategies will be played two times. The first time, listen to the discourse markers that organize the information. They are partially written below. Fill in the missing words as you hear them.

What I _____ to say is there are …

It goes _____ saying that a prepared student …

Judging is _____ a disadvantage …

I _____ to stress that successful …

pertaining _____ the topic …

Second Listening: Listen and Take Notes Use the space below to take notes and write important information. Don't worry about correct spelling or writing complete sentences. If you are comfortable using note-taking symbols, practice them in this activity.

Compare Notes

With a partner, answer the questions below. If you have different opinions about an answer, look at each other's notes and try to come up with the best answer. Write down the differences from your original notes. When you are finished, compare your answers with those of the rest of the class.

1. The speaker talks about many strategies that students can use to become better note takers and students. What are the two items he mentions that students should do before the lecture begins?

    _____

    _____

    Different notes: _____

2. What are the specific benefits of doing these two things?

    _____

    _____

    Different notes: _____

3. What does the speaker say that students should do if they disagree with what the lecturer is saying? (More than one answer is possible.)

    _____

    _____

    Different notes: _____

4. What three things do teachers do to signal that the information they are presenting is important?

    _____

    _____

    _____

    Different notes: _____

Think Critically: About You

Read the questions and answer them in the space provided. When you have finished, share your answers with the class.

1. Think about your own "student habits." How do they compare to the lecturer's suggestions?

    _____

    _____

2. Was there any information presented in the lecture that you were not familiar with? _____ If so, which strategies are you willing to try?

    _____

    _____

3. Is there anything in the lecture that you disagree with? _____ If so, explain your reason(s) and give other suggestions for being a better note taker.

_____

_____

_____

SPEAKING ● **Interviewing**

ACTIVITY **13**

Conduct Interviews: Analyze Study Skills and Academic Goals

Interviewing is a valuable skill for gathering information. The effectiveness of an interview rests mainly on the quality of the questions and on how well you record the answers. This activity will allow you to analyze study skills and higher education preferences.

Task

Create a list of ten questions to ask a classmate about his or her academic goals and study skills. Use the strategies below to help you write your questions and conduct the interview. Then share three interview answers with the class.

Interviewing Strategies

1. Bring a notebook and pen to the interview.

2. Avoid asking **yes** or **no** questions (Do you study in the library?). They limit the information you receive. Instead, ask open-ended questions beginning with **what**, **who**, **where**, **why**, and **how** (Where do you study, and what do you like about that place?). These questions will encourage the person you are interviewing to give longer answers.

3. If the person does not understand the question, restate it another way or give an example of how you would answer the question.

4. Be careful of your tone of voice. Do not make judgments about the person being interviewed. A question such as "Do you think you're not good enough to enter a university?" is not appropriate.

5. You can use some of the following topics to create different kinds of questions, but make sure to add questions of your own.
   • the person's study skills
   • where the person usually sits in the classroom and why
   • academic subjects that the person is interested in
   • how often the person reviews notes or studies
   • what types of speakers the person enjoys listening to
   • the benefits of community colleges
   • the benefits of universities

6. Make sure you leave enough space between each question so that you can record the complete answer.

SAMPLE INTERVIEW FORM

Interviewer name:	Date:
Interviewee name:	Subject:

1. How often do you take notes in class?

2. What is your favorite method of taking notes?

3.

4.

NOTE: See Appendix 3, page 133, for sample forms for evaluating oral presentations.

 ACTIVITY 14

Expand Your Interview Questions

Now that you know how to write interview questions, try writing between five and ten questions to ask a staff or faculty member on your campus. The questions can be about facts and statistics about the college, about the person's opinion on a certain subject, or about another topic.

SENTENCE COMPLETION FROM PAGE 9

"John F. Kennedy was assassinated. <u>On the other hand,</u> Winston Churchill died of a stroke."

The two deaths were different. By hearing the discourse marker phrase "on the other hand," the listener can guess that the information that follows is going to be in contrast to the previous information that came before.

 For more activities and information, go to the *Key Concepts 1* website at *elt.heinle.com/keyconcepts*.

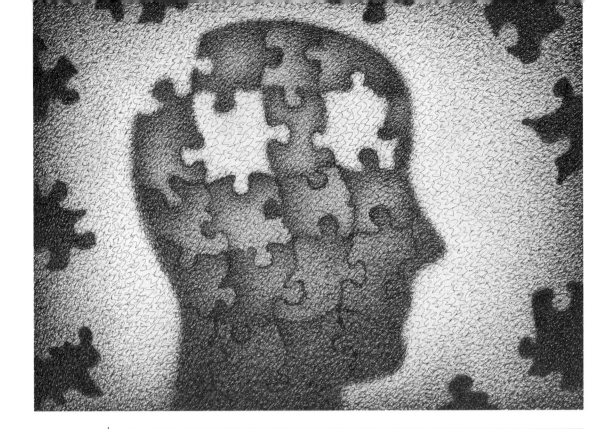

2 • From the Social Sciences: Psychology

PSY 101
Introduction to Psychology (3)
This course studies the major areas of psychological science. Topics include human social behavior, personality, psychological disorders and treatment, memory, human development, biological influences, and research methods. Other topics covered: sensation, perception, states of consciousness, thinking, intelligence, language, emotion, stress and health, cross-cultural psychology, and applied psychology. *Offered: year-round*

Psychology courses are some of the most popular courses in community colleges and universities. Students are generally required to take at least one course in the social sciences, and psychology is the number one choice. Read the description of a psychology course.

Locate a course description for an introductory psychology course from a community college or university catalog. Compare it with the description on the left. What similarities do the two courses have? What are the differences?

Students in psychology courses have many different tasks: reading the textbook, understanding the information, listening to lectures, taking notes, writing essays and papers, engaging in class discussions, and making presentations.

This chapter will help you understand some **key concepts** of psychology, such as

- types of psychology
- research methods in psychology
- the use of surveys in data collection

You will also practice some academic skills for success.

Get Ready to Listen

ACTIVITY **1**

Brainstorming and Discussion

Psychology is defined as the branch of knowledge that deals with the human mind. It is connected to the examination of mental and behavioral qualities.

A. On a separate piece of paper, answer the question below. Do not write your name on the paper.

> *Question:* **What kind of person am I?**

As you answer, consider the following areas of your life: personality, interests, goals, successes, and family role.

B. Split into groups of three or four. Place all the answers together and mix them up. Have one person choose a piece of paper and read the information to the group. Can you guess which person is being described?

C. Classify your group's answers in the following chart.

CATEGORY	DESCRIPTION	STUDENT NAMES
Personality		
Interests		
Goals		
Successes		
Family role		

Read for Inference

With a partner or a small group, read the conversations and answer the questions orally.

A. Read the following conversation from a beginning level English text.

> *Bob:* Hi Linda, do you want to go have lunch?
> *Linda:* Sure, Bob. That's a great idea!

How does Linda feel about Bob's suggestion? Linda's response to the question is what many people would expect to hear. However, sometimes in natural communication we have to infer, or "read between the lines," for the true meaning. We must make a guess as to how people really feel based on what they say and how they say it.

B. Read the next conversation. What is the second speaker really saying?

> *Bob:* Hi Linda, do you want to go have lunch?
> *Linda:* I had a huge breakfast, Bob.

Notice how Linda does not say *yes* or *no*. Instead, she explains something that she did earlier in the day. Do you think that Bob and Linda will have lunch together today? Why or why not?

C. Now read the next conversation. What does Linda mean?

> *Bob:* Hey Linda, can I borrow a few dollars? I'm broke.
> *Linda:* My car payment is due tomorrow, Bob.

Will Linda give Bob money? Why or why not?

Listen and Respond

ACTIVITY 3

Listen to Conversations

Listen to the short conversations. Answer the questions you hear.

Conversation 1:

1. a. employer—employee
    b. two friends
    c. mother—son
    d. two work colleagues

2. a. nervous
    b. very happy
    c. relieved
    d. angry

Conversation 2:

3. a. employer—employee
    b. two friends
    c. mother—daughter
    d. two sisters

4. a. It is her fault for failing the test.
    b. The test was too difficult.
    c. She didn't understand the information.
    d. She wants to take the test again.

Conversation 3:

5. a. He agrees with the comment.
    b. He doesn't believe the comment.
    c. He thinks the comment might be true.
    d. He wants to check with the teacher.

6. a. a statement
    b. a question
    c. an exclamation
    d. a quote

Conversation 4:

7. a. husband—wife
    b. professor—student
    c. uncle—niece
    d. classmates

8. a. She thinks the man is crazy.
    b. She thinks he is a good student
    c. She doesn't want to give him her notes.
    d. She is jealous of the man.

Vocabulary

Academic Word List

Practice reading and saying aloud these vocabulary words. How many of the words do you already know?

1. **analyze** [ăn´ ə līz´] v. to separate something into parts in order to determine what it is or how it works; to examine in detail

   I don't understand some people's behavior. It's very difficult for me to analyze.

2. **available** [ə vā´ lə bəl] adj. capable of being obtained; at hand and ready for use

   Historical psychology classes are available to university students here.

3. **benefit** [běn´ ə fĭt] n. something that is of help; an advantage. v. to be helpful to someone or something

   The biggest benefit of crying is releasing your emotions. (n)
   Daily exercise benefits the mind as well as the body. (v)

4. **evident** [ěv´ ĭ dənt] adj. easily seen or understood

   It is evident that Marcy is not acting like herself.

5. **involve** [ĭn vŏlv´] v. to contain something as a part; include

   Becoming a psychologist involves getting an advanced degree.

6. **method** [měth´ əd] n. a regular or orderly way of doing something

   For me, the best method for understanding my actions is to keep a personal journal.

7. **research** [rē´ sûrch´] n. careful study of a certain subject. [rĭ sûrch´] v. to do research on something; investigate

   Harry spent five hours in the library doing research on the effects of divorce on teenagers. (n)
   Psychologists are researching the emotional reasons for childhood obesity. (v)

8. **structure** [strŭk´ chər] n. something made of a number of parts. v. to give form or arrangement to something

   I have a hard time understanding old-fashioned family structures where the wife does not work outside of the home. (n)
   The university counselor likes to structure his workshops with lots of peer interaction. (v)

9. **theory** [thē´ ə rē] or [thîr´ ē] n. a statement designed to explain an event; an assumption based on limited information

   There are many theories about why people act in destructive ways.

10. **vary** [vâr´ ē] or [văr´ ē] v. to be different from others of its type

    Displays of affection vary from culture to culture.

Vocabulary Practice

Complete each sentence with a word from the Academic Word List . You may have to change the singular form of the word.

available	involve	structure	method	theory
vary	analyze	research	benefit	evident

1. I want to study psychology because I always _____ everything: my behavior, my actions, and my thoughts.

2. My psychologist has a _____ that I am afraid to grow up. I think she might be right.

3. The only _____ appointment date with Dr. Schwartz is one month from now.

4. My new job doesn't pay very well, but it offers lots of _____ such as three weeks' vacation and free health insurance and counseling.

5. In their research on childhood behavior, the researchers looked at the family _____ of each of the children.

6. Many people say that if you _____ the direction you drive to work or school, life can seem more interesting.

7. Because no one in the class knew the answer to the professor's question, she asked us to _____ it on the Internet after class.

8. There are so many _____ for improving your memory: copying information down, repeating it out loud, practicing it every day, etc.

9. Look at my grade on last week's quiz: I got a 60%. It's _____ that I didn't study.

10. Becoming a successful independent psychiatrist _____ years of study, internships, and, eventually, the money to open a private clinic.

Taking Notes: Outlines

Using Outlines

In Chapter 1, you learned about the importance of the note-taking process: observing, recording, and reviewing. One method of recording is using an outline. Because teachers who prepare lectures well tend to speak in organized and logical patterns, it can be easy for students to use the outline format when taking notes. The outline form is similar to what students use when they prepare to write an academic paper.

Outline Example 1

Study this partial outline on the birth of psychology.

The main points are made using roman numerals (I, II, III, etc.).

Supporting ideas follow underneath with letters (A, B, C, etc.).

If supporting ideas have more specific information, then the numbers (1, 2, 3, etc.) are used.

HISTORY OF PSYCHOLOGY
I. Modern birth of psychology
   A. 1879
   B. Wilhelm Wundt began lab
      1. formal research lab
      2. University of Leipzig, Germany
II. Psychology in history
   A. Ancient Greeks
      1. Socrates
      2. Plato
      3. Aristotle
   B. 1700s
      1. Empiricism
      2. rational psychology

Outline Example 2

Below is the same partial outline using different signals to show main ideas and supporting details.

Main point of the lecture

Supporting ideas use bullets (dots)

More specific information (dashes)

Modern birth of psychology
   • 1879
   • Wilhelm Wundt began lab
      – formal research lab
      – University of Leipzig
Psychology in history
   • Ancient Greeks
      – Socrates
      – Plato
      – Aristotle
   • 1700s
      – Empiricism
      – Rational psychology

Listen and Respond

Listen and Use Strategies You Learned

First Listening: Listen for Vocabulary You will hear a mini-lecture played two times. The first time, listen for vocabulary from the Academic Word List. Number the vocabulary words in the order that you hear them. Write the number above the vocabulary word.

structure	analyze	theory	evident	vary
research	involve	benefit	available	methods

Second Listening: Listen and Outline Listen to the mini-lecture again. Concentrate on the information being presented and how it's organized. Fill in the missing information in the outline below.

Fields of Psychology

   I. Introduction

      A. number of psychologists: _____

      B. analyzing human behavior

      C. career opportunities _____ greatly

  II. _____

      A. _____

         1. research

            a. _____

         2. study

            a. learning

            b. _____

            c. _____

         3. also called experimental psychology

      B. Biological psychology

         1. _____

         2. how the brain controls physical movements of the body

      C. _____

         1. _____

         2. Who do we like? Why?

 III. Conclusion

      A. Small sample of psychology jobs

         1. many careers for many people

         2. _____

Answer Questions about the Mini-Lecture

Review your outline from Activity 5. Then circle the letter of the correct answer to the questions about the mini-lecture.

1. How many specific jobs are described in the mini-lecture?
   a. half a million
   b. half
   c. a million

2. What is the main idea of this lecture?
   a. some psychology jobs are better than others
   b. experimental psychology is the same as cognitive psychology
   c. there are many types of psychology

3. Which type of psychology study focuses on the structure of the brain and movements of the body?
   a. social psychology
   b. cognitive psychology
   c. biological psychology

4. If you had a problem getting along with your boss, which type of psychologist might help you?
   a. social psychologist
   b. cognitive psychologist
   c. biological psychologist

5. According to the lecture, which field of psychology does NOT mention activities connected to mental (brain) processes?
   a. social psychology
   b. cognitive psychology
   c. biological psychology

Pronunciation Differences

In spoken English, some words are pronounced more than one way. One common example is the pronunciation of the article *the*. This article can be pronounced in two ways in English.

ACTIVITY **7**

Listen for Pronunciation Differences

A. Listen to the following phrases and sentences as they are read. Pay careful attention to the pronunciation of the word *the*. If the word is pronounced with a reduced sound [ə] (schwa), as in the word *but*, circle the symbol [ə] above the word. If the word *the* is pronounced with a long sound [ē], as in the word *beat*, circle the symbol [ē].

1. What psychologists must do, in effect, is to describe a phenomenon, to make some predictions about it, and finally to introduce some control
[ə] [ē]
over the variables.

                               [ə] [ē]
2. These three things, when done properly, let the observing psychologist
[ə] [ē]
explain the phenomenon with some confidence.

[ə] [ē]
3. The most common ways are using …

       [ə] [ē]
4. A lot of the information we now have …

[ə] [ē]
5. The next point I'd like to cover is …

                    [ə] [ē]
6. The group must be representative of the overall population.

[ə] [ē]   [ə] [ē]
7. The answers will not be representative of the general population.

[ə] [ē]
8. The results will not be valid.

B. Study the eight phrases and sentences again. Why do you think the word *the* is pronounced two different ways?

_____

_____

To check your answers, look on page 38.

Discourse Markers: Various Functions

Study the following discourse markers, which signal a transition in information. You will hear many of these phrases in the extended lecture.

Function	Phrase
Introducing information	Today, we're going to discuss …
Listing	To begin with … The next point I'd like to cover
Giving examples	For instance, Take X, for example
Emphasizing	In effect, This goes to show that
Clarifying	Basically, In other words,
Classifying	There are X categories of Y
Concluding	To sum up,

NOTE: For a more complete list of discourse markers, see Appendix 6, page 140.

Vocabulary

Academic Word List

Practice reading and saying aloud these vocabulary words. How many do you already know?

1. **area** [âr´ ē ə] n. range of activity or study

   There are many different jobs in the <u>area</u> of psychology.

2. **consist** (of) [kən sĭst´] v. to be made up or composed of

   The hospital's counseling sessions <u>consist</u> of thirty minutes of individual work and twenty minutes with a group.

3. **create** [krē āt´] v. to bring something into being; cause to exist

   Some criminal psychologists <u>create</u> profiles of potential offenders.

4. **data** [dā´ tə] or [dăt´ ə] n. information, especially when it is to be analyzed or used as the basis for a decision

   After two years of research, Sonia decided that her research <u>data</u> was ready to be analyzed.

5. **define** [dĭ fīn´] v. to state the exact meaning of a word or phrase

   The dictionary <u>defines</u> *psychology* as the science of minds, emotions, and behaviors.

6. **identify** [ĭ dĕn´ tə fī´] v. to establish or recognize somebody or something as a certain person or thing

   My dog can <u>identify</u> me by my voice; he doesn't need to see me.

7. **major** [mā´ jər] adj. greater or more important than others. n. field of study; v. to study or specialize in a subject

   Sigmund Freud's <u>major</u> claim to fame was his research on the *id* and the *ego*. (adj)
   I've changed my <u>major</u> from accounting to behavioral psychology. (n)
   Many people who <u>major</u> in psychology go into clinical research. (v)

8. **occur** [ə kûr´] v. to happen without planning

   Increased interest in psychology <u>occurred</u> in the nineteenth century.

9. **process** [prŏs´ ĕs´] n. a series of actions, changes, or functions leading to a desired result. v. to put something through a fixed series of steps

   The <u>process</u> of understanding ourselves as human beings is often over analyzed. (n)
   It took the doctor's office only ten minutes to <u>process</u> my paperwork. (v)

10. **source** [sôrs] n. a person or thing that supplies information

    The teacher said that we have to use at least four <u>sources</u> in our psychology paper.

ACTIVITY 8   *Vocabulary Practice*

Read the paragraph below. Then complete the paragraph with words from the box. Do not use a word more than once. You will not use all of the words.

define	identify	process	source	major
consist	occur	data	area	create

Have you ever heard the phrase "critical thinking"? We can (1) _____ *critical thinking* as a (2) _____ (or series of steps) used to make judgments. These judgments must (3) _____ of well-supported evidence. For example, if people believe that something is true because "everyone knows it is true," this is not critical thinking. Some advertisers, politicians, and others (4) _____ this message because they want your money, vote, etc. When people believe in this information, problems (5) _____ and people can lose things that are precious to them such as money, power, and free will. People who think critically ask themselves questions to (6) _____ the claim as believable or not. The first question is, "What are they asking me to believe?" Another question is, "Do I have any (7) _____ or evidence that can help me make a decision?" People can also think about different reasons or methods of explaining something. Critical thinking is important in scientific research because it breaks the (8) _____ idea into smaller parts.

Special Vocabulary to Know

Studying these key words will help you as you listen to the extended lecture.

phenomenon [fĭ **nŏm´** ə nŏn´] n. an occurrence or fact that can be perceived by the senses or by instruments

variables [vâr´ ē ə bəlz] n. elements that change

confidence [kŏn´ fĭ dəns] n. a feeling of assurance, especially self-assurance

Listen and Respond

ACTIVITY **9**

Listen and Use Strategies You Learned

First Listening: Listen for Discourse Markers You will hear an extended lecture played two times. The first time, listen for discourse markers that organize the information. If you hear a phrase from the list below, put a check mark next to it. You will hear seven of these phrases.

_____ Today, we're going to discuss …   _____ To begin with …

_____ The next point I'd like to cover   _____ For instance,

_____ Take psychology, for example   _____ In effect,

_____ This goes to show that   _____ Basically,

_____ In other words,   _____ There are many categories of

_____ To sum up,

Second Listening: Listen and Take Notes Listen to the extended lecture again. On a separate piece of paper, take notes on the most important information. Use the outline technique that you practiced on p. 28.

ACTIVITY ⑩   ***Answer Questions about the Extended Lecture***

In small groups, answer the questions that follow. When you are finished, put your group's answers on the board, and discuss them with the rest of the class.

1. What three things must psychologists do in order to explain a phenomenon?

   _____

   _____

2. How do psychologists collect information?

   _____

   _____

3. Which method uses "people-watching" to get information?

   _____

   _____

4. Which method uses many different categories to get information?

   _____

   _____

   Extra question: Can you give one specific category used in this method?

   _____

5. Why must surveys have a "representative" population?

   _____

   _____

6. What will be discussed in next week's lecture?

   _____

   _____

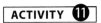
Think Critically: Evaluate and Compare Information from the Lecture

Working with a partner, read the question below and fill in the chart. When you have finished, compare your answers with those of the rest of the class.

In your opinion, what are the advantages and disadvantages of each type of observation tool mentioned in the lecture?

NATURALISTIC OBSERVATIONS

Advantages   Disadvantages

CASE STUDIES

Advantages   Disadvantages

SURVEYS

Advantages   Disadvantages

Survey: Strategies for Working in Groups

1. College students are often asked to work together in small groups and reach a consensus, which means an agreement or compromise. Group activity is beneficial because it

   - allows everyone to participate in a discussion.

   - gives students the opportunity to listen to others' opinions.

   - develops social skills.

   - allows for more information to be covered in a shorter period of time.

   - practices consensus building.

2. However, working together and sharing information are successful only if certain rules are followed. Students should always be courteous of others' opinions, give everyone a chance to speak, and participate actively. Decide what each member of the group will do.

   - Will each member work on a separate item?

   - Will you work in pairs within your team?

   - Will one person manage the entire project?

   - How will you decide if the survey and the observation methods are appropriate?

ACTIVITY 12 *Survey: Come up with a Technique to Study Twins*

Read the following situation about two women who are twins.

Lisa and Janice are identical twins, aged 24. However, they did not grow up in the same house. They were separated at birth and grew up with two different families. One family lived in California, and the other lived in Texas.

Lisa and Janice have recently found each other. Of course they look alike, with the same color hair, eyes, and skin. In fact, they even share the same hairstyle. It is obvious that the twins are similar physically, but do they share the same personality?

Task

In small groups, create methods of testing the following hypothesis:

"Twins who grow up separately share the same basic personality traits."

To get as much information about Lisa's and Janice's personalities as you can, prepare two techniques discussed in the extended lecture—naturalistic observations and surveys. Develop these methods for collecting important personality traits about twins separated at birth.

Follow these guidelines to prepare to collect information.

1. *Survey:* Develop survey questions for identical twins separated as children. Ask about different areas of their lives, such as basic values, interests, and feelings. Use the Sample Survey Scales for ideas about how to evaluate the answers to the survey questions you write.

> **Sample Survey Scales**
>
> 1. Descriptive words
>
>   Question of frequency: How often do you …?
>
>   *always   frequently   sometimes   rarely   never*
>
>   Question of emotion: How do you feel about …?
>
>   *happy   interested   not interested   angry*
>
> 2. Numerical scale (1 = *not interested* and 10 = *very interested*)
>
>   1   2   3   4   5   6   7   8   9   10

In the space below, write your survey questions using one or more of the survey scales above.

2. *Naturalistic Observation:* In what situations would you observe a pair of twins? Make a list of places, environments, and situations that you think would help you gain some knowledge about twins' behavior.

As a group, create at least two separate surveys and observation lists. When you have finished, share your scientific methods of studying twins with the rest of the class.

ACTIVITY **13**   ***Compare Psychology Syllabi Online***

Using a search engine of your choice, type in *psychology syllabus* in the search field. Compare at least four different syllabi pertaining to psychology. Is the information presented similar? Do you notice some key concepts that appear in more than one syllabus? Take notes and share your findings with the class.

PRONUNCIATION RULE:

(From page 30.) The pronunciation of the word *the* depends on the sound that follows it. If *the* is followed by a consonant sound, the vowel sound in *the* is reduced [ə]. However, if the word following *the* begins with a vowel sound, *the* is pronounced with a long [ē] sound like *thee.*

 For more activities and information, go to the *Key Concepts 1* website at *elt.heinle.com/keyconcepts.*

MAR 203

Introduction to International Marketing (3)

This is a required course for all international business students. This course concentrates on the advances in marketing through the Internet, the political and legal requirements of various countries, and cultural and political realities for the international entrepreneur. The student will gain a basic understanding of market channeling, research, and market entry procedures and strategies.

3 • From Business: International Trade and Marketing

Business is one of the most popular majors among community college and university students. The course description above fills one of the requirements for students interested in majoring in business. Read the description for a class in international marketing.

Now find a course description for a similar course from a local community college or university catalog. What similarities do the two courses have? What are the differences?

This chapter will help you understand some of the **key concepts** of international trade and marketing such as

- the important elements of marketing a product internationally
- the effects of the industrial revolution on business
- the relationship between international business and the Internet
- the benefits and problems that arise from the rapidly developing global marketplace

You will also practice some academic skills for success.

Get Ready to Listen

ACTIVITY **1**

Brainstorming and Discussion

A. Product Origins

Working with a partner, read the list of products below. In your opinion, which country or countries are best known for producing the items? Try to answer as many as you can. When you are finished, compare your answers with the rest of the class.

1. champagne: ___France___
2. cotton: _____
3. automobiles: _____
4. computer chips: _____
5. cell phones: _____
6. ornamental rugs: _____
7. diamonds: _____
8. leather goods: _____
9. sporting equipment: _____
10. caviar: _____
11. silk: _____

B. U.S. Imports

Marketing is the concept and practice of advertising and selling things on a large scale. Many goods are sold between countries.

Think of products that are imported to the United States. With a partner, write them in the spaces below. If you can't think of any imported products, list products from other countries that you think people in the United States would like, such as a tasty food or drink, fashionable clothes, or electronic equipment.

_____

_____

_____

_____

_____

_____

_____

_____

_____

_____

_____

C. Whose Product Is Better?

Now choose from the list in Part B one product that is the same as or similar to a product that is made in the United States. Which do you think is better, the product made in the United States or the one made in another country? Are there any cost differences? In the spaces below, write the reasons why you think one country's product is better than the other country's product.

Product: _____

Which is better? _____ Why? _____

_____

_____

_____

D. Compare Information

Share the information you wrote with your classmates. Put some lists on the board and compare one product to another. Try using the comparative form.

NOTE: Comparative adjectives are formed in the following way:

- Add *-er* to the adjective if it has one syllable and follow it with *than*.

- Add *more* (or *less*) to it if it has two or more syllables (there are exceptions).

- Add *-ier* to it if it ends in *y* (drop the *y*).

  My sister is *closer than* I am to getting a degree in economics.
  The differences in international law make business *more difficult*.
  The Internet has made doing business *easier*.

Comparatives can also be used with adverbs. In this case, the words *more* or *less* are used before the adverb.

  Goods are marketed *more widely* in the global marketplace.
  Products were sold *less quickly* before the Internet was created.

Understand Time Relationships

Many conversations discuss the elements of time. In English, there are many ways to tell a listener about when something happened or will happen. All of the short conversations you will hear in Listening 1 contain a reference to time. Study the timeline and charts in Activity 2. Then practice using time phrases to prepare for listening in Activity 3.

 **Explain Events in Relation to Time**

1. Study the time expressions in the box.

yesterday	today	tomorrow
the day **before** yesterday	the day **after** tomorrow	
a week **ago** (7 days before now)	**in** a week (in 7 days)/a week **from** now	
	in two weeks, three weeks, etc	
3 days **ago**	**in** 3 days/3 days **from** now	

NOTE: *Last* means sometime in the week **before** this week; *next* means sometime in the week **after** this week.

last week	**next** week (late next week, early next week)
last Monday (or Tuesday, etc.)	**next** Monday (or Tuesday, etc.)

NOTE: Use *the* to mean "the one before now" with things other than days or dates *or* when you mean the **final** one.

> What **did** we do in *the* last class? (past—the one before now)
> What **will** we do in *the* last class? (future—**the final** class)

2. Study the timeline. The line of numbers shows the dates and the line of letters shows the days of the week (M is Monday, etc.). *Today* on this chart is April 1.

MARCH												Today	APRIL													
M	T	W	Th	F	S	Su	M	T	W	Th	F	S	Su	M	T	W	Th	F	S	Su	M	T	W	Th	F
21	22	23	24	25	26	27	28	29	30	31	1	2	3	4	5	6	7	8	9	10	11	12	13	14	15

LAST week **THIS** week **NEXT** week two weeks **FROM NOW**

NOTE: In the United States, the week begins on Sunday.

3. Complete each sentence with a time expression from the box. Use the timeline above. More than one answer may be possible.

1. I saw Michael on the twenty-ninth. _I saw him three days ago._

2. The test will be on the eighth. The test will be _____.

3. I spoke to Maria on the thirty-first. I spoke to her _____.

4. Bill saw the movie on the thirtieth. Bill saw the movie _____.

5. I will start my vacation on the fifth. I will start it _____.

6. She will go home in four days. She will go home early _____.

7. You must hand in the report by next Tuesday. It's _____ day you can hand in the report.

8. I remember _____ time I was in New York.

9. I will see her on the thirteenth. I will see her _____.

10. The guest speaker came on the twenty-fifth. She came _____.

Listen and Respond

Listen to Conversations

Listen to the short conversations. Pay attention to the expressions, using the timeline on page 42. Then answer the question about each conversation. Circle the letter of the correct answer.

Conversation 1: When will the test be?
- a. next week
- b. the day after tomorrow
- c. tomorrow
- d. next Friday

Conversation 2: When is the last exam?
- a. the last week of the semester
- b. last week
- c. after five chapters
- d. before the reports

Conversation 3: When was the homework given?
- a. this Tuesday
- b last week
- c. yesterday
- d. Thursday of the week before last week

Conversation 4: When is the man going to the seminar?

    a. this weekend

    b. the weekend after this one

    c. two weeks from now

    d. the end of this week

Conversation 5: When did the woman go on the tour?

    a. sometime last semester

    b. a few days ago

    c. yesterday

    d. at some time earlier in the semester

Conversation 6: When is the deadline for the report?

    a. tomorrow

    b. next week

    c. the first day of class next week

    d. Wednesday

LISTENING 2 • Mini-Lecture: International Trade

Taking Notes: Word Maps

Using Word Maps

One way of taking good notes is to use word maps. A word map consists of connected circles, each with important information in it. These circles connect ideas using lines from one circle to another.

ACTIVITY 4

Take Notes in a Word Map

Below is a short reading followed by a partially completed word map. As you read the paragraph, notice the transition words (discourse markers such as, *first, second, third,* and *in addition*). They will help you connect the material correctly. Then complete the word map.

Different conditions can have important effects on global marketing strategies. First, a country's population size affects the market. Countries with larger populations usually have lower product prices. These larger countries also have more company offices and salespeople, whereas smaller countries use independent distributors. Second is the level of income for people in the country. If people cannot afford to pay the normal price for a product, then a price change must be made. Also, convenient access to credit must be available in such countries. In addition, if a poor country's population has underdeveloped technical skills, the company may need to simplify a product's design to market it in that country. Third are social and cultural factors. The traditional tastes of a country's people may influence sales—a product that is popular in one country may not sell well in another. Last is how the language of the country affects sales. One example of this is the difficulty for Western software companies that sell in Asia. Translations of advertisements into certain combinations of Kanji, a writing system used widely in Asia, are unacceptable or confusing in various countries in the Far East for both political and cultural reasons.

Word Map

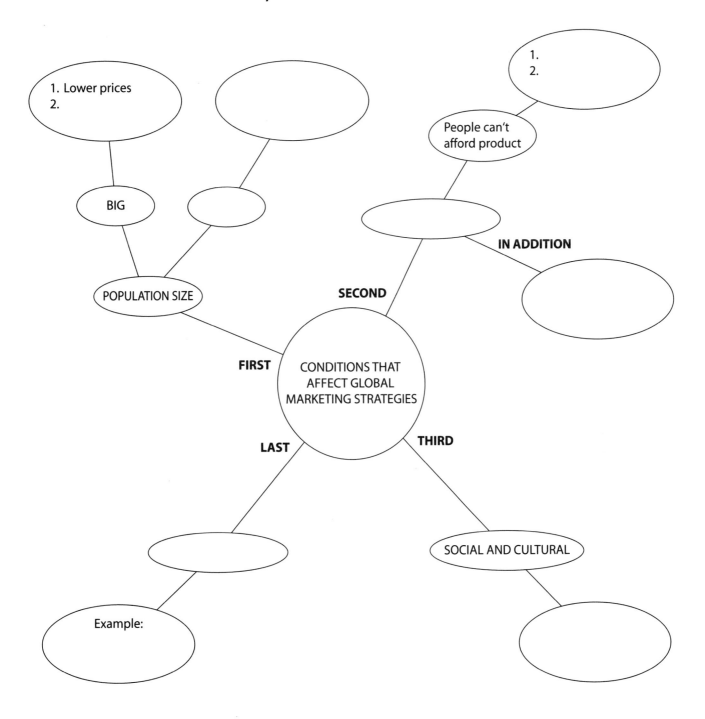

Vocabulary

Academic Word List

Practice reading and saying aloud these vocabulary words. How many of the words do you already know?

1. **commission** [kə **mĭsh´** ən] n. Money in the form of a fee or a percentage of a price paid to a salesperson or agent for services; v. to place an order for something

   The dealer's <u>commission</u> on the $500 sale was $50. (n)
   The company <u>commissioned</u> the architect to design its new building. (v)

2. **compute** [kəm **pyo͞ot´**] v. to find (a result, an answer, or a solution) by mathematics; calculate

   The bank <u>computes</u> interest on savings accounts.

3. **contract** [**kŏn´** trăkt´] n. an agreement between two or more persons or groups, especially one that is written and enforceable by law. [kən **trăkt´**] or [**kŏn´** trăkt´] v. to arrange or settle by formal agreement

   The agent has the <u>contract</u> to sell the new house. (n)
   The music company <u>contracted</u> her to do a new CD. (v)

4. **distribute** [dĭ **strĭb´** yo͞ot] v. to divide and give something out in regular amounts or shares

   That company <u>distributes</u> fresh vegetables to other parts of the country.

5. **export** [ĭk **spôrt´**] or [**ĕk´** spôrt´] v. to send or transport a good to another country. [**ĕk´** spôrt´] n. a product that is exported

   My uncle's company <u>exports</u> most of its products to Europe. (v)
   <u>Exports</u> of steel have fallen in the last ten years. (n)

6. **finance** [fə **năns´**] or [**fī´** năns´] n. the science of the management of money or other financial assets; v. to provide or obtain funds or capital for something

   An economist is a specialist in <u>finance</u>. (n)
   The International Monetary Fund (IMF) <u>finances</u> developing countries. (v)

7. **invest** [ĭn **vĕst´**] v. to put money into something, such as a business or stocks, in order to earn interest or make a profit

   Many people <u>invest</u> their money in the stock market.

8. **obtain** [əb **tān´**] v. to get or acquire
   She <u>obtained</u> her driver's license last month.

9. **purchase** [**pûr´** chĭs] v. to get something in exchange for money; to buy. n. something that is bought

   She <u>purchased</u> a new home. (v)
   A house is the biggest <u>purchase</u> many people make in their lives. (n)

10. **resource** [**rē´** sôrs´] or [rĭ **sôrs´**] n. something that is a source of wealth to a country; something that can be used for support or help

    That country has no big energy <u>resources</u>, such as gas or coal.

Vocabulary Practice

Rearrange the words in each item to make a sentence. The first word of each sentence has been circled for you. More than one correct answer may be possible.

1. about businessman know doesn't finance (that) much

   <u>That businessman doesn't know much about finance.</u>

2. obtain some (our) new company to software licenses needs

   <u>Our</u>

   _____

3. exports electronics (Japan) and many has car

   <u>Japan</u>

   _____

4. contract price unless won't sign the you the (we) lower

   <u>We</u>

   _____

5. doesn't business have distribute (that) enough to products its trucks

   <u>That</u>

   _____

6. company invest money a (I've) new energy my decided solar to in

   <u>I've</u>

   _____

7. resource modern most (oil) the necessary world's is

   <u>Oil</u>

   _____

8. should save fewer more purchase things money (you) and

   <u>You</u>

   _____

9. a (she) the commission for she sells receives products

   <u>She</u>

   _____

10. me a and will compute (give) the I moment costs

    <u>Give</u>

    _____

Listen and Respond

Listen and Use Strategies You Learned

First Listening: Listen and Connect Words

You will hear a mini-lecture about international trade played two times. Review the two columns of words below. Say the words in the left column to yourself. Among them are the vocabulary words from the list above and the discourse markers you will study soon. Listen to the mini-lecture once. Draw a line to connect the words in the left column with the words in the right column that immediately follow them in the lecture.

Part I

1. As we know   within countries

2. second   information

3. distributed   of a distant country

4. exported   countries have traded

5. I'd like to emphasize   between countries

6. obtain   was the increased speed

7. resources   that we are

8. invest   in other countries

Part II

9. purchase   needed materials

10. commissions   computed

11. costs are   it's time to begin

12. contracts   in a few minutes

13. finance   this was impossible

14. whereas   is sent

15. moving on   are signed

Listen to the mini-lecture again. Complete the word map using vocabulary from the
Academic Word List on p. 46 and other information you hear.

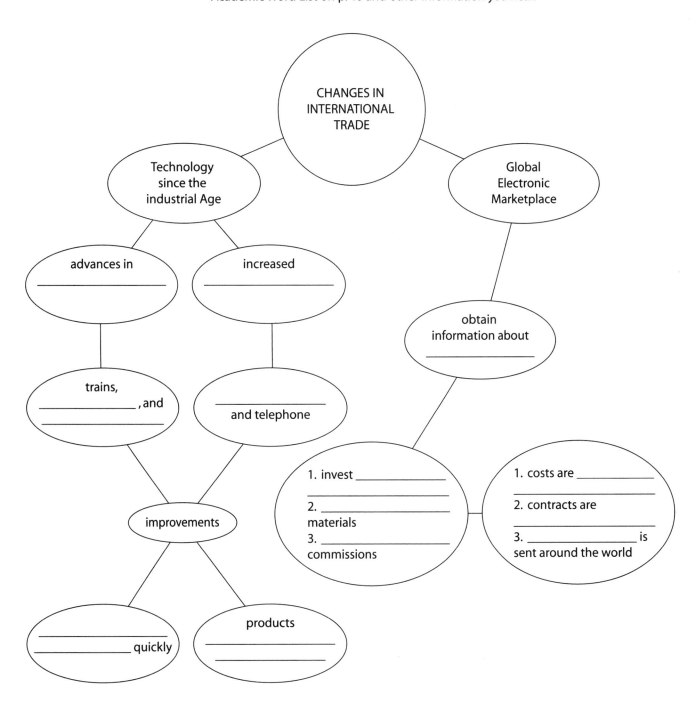

Answer Questions about the Mini-Lecture

Use the word map from Activity 6 to answer the questions about the mini-lecture.

1. What were the three forms of improved transportation resulting from the Industrial Revolution?

   _____

   _____

   _____

2. How was distribution improved by the inventions in question 1?

   _____

   _____

3. Name two communications inventions of the Industrial Revolution that made business deals easier and faster.

   _____

   _____

4. How has the computerized marketplace made business easier?

   _____

   _____

ACTIVITY **8**

Think Critically: Compare Exporting Methods

With a partner, study the chart on the following page. On the left, you will see the basic set of steps needed to produce and export merchandise. The blank spaces to the right are for the materials and methods necessary to carry out the export process. The column labeled *1880* represents exporting in that year. The column labeled *The Twenty-first Century* shows today's common procedures for exporting a product.

Use the list below to complete the chart on page 51. When you have filled out as much information as you can, compare your answers with those of the rest of the class. The first one has been done for you.

- handmade signs; word of mouth; locally distributed posters
- ships, planes, trucks
- hand delivery of payment; use of couriers (usually on horseback) to deliver payment
- TV, radio, computer ads
- ~~manual labor; primitive machinery~~
- using market research to set prices; setting different prices based on the quantity of goods purchased
- researching in trade magazines and industry associations for buyers; doing independent research via computer searches; contacting foreign and local wholesalers
- direct deposit by computer; checks; mail delivery
- ~~automated machines; outsourcing tasks~~
- prices generally set by the seller because of little competition
- using connections overseas such as family and friends; traveling abroad to study the market and make preliminary contacts
- ship, steam engine trains

TASK	YEAR	
Exporting Cotton Textiles	1880	The Twenty-first Century
1. manufacturing the goods	• manual labor • primitive machinery	• automated machines • outsourcing tasks
2. advertising		
3. finding buyers		
4. negotiating price		
5. exporting merchandise		
6. receiving payments		

Academic Word List Review: Word Forms

The following sentences use the Academic Word List vocabulary from page 46, but most of the words are used as a different part of speech. The changes in these word forms have been supplied at the end of the blanks. If the word doesn't change it will say **no change**. Note that you may need to drop the final *e* of some verbs to make them nouns.

   Example: produce/production

More than one answer is possible in some sentences.

1. We need to __contract__ (*no change*) a company to clean our office at night. (verb)

2. Our _____**ment** in technology stocks has made us a lot of money. (noun)

3. She always finds the thing she needs for her company. She is very _____**ful**. (adj.)

4. It's a great idea, but how will we be able to _____ (*no change*) it? We don't have that much money. (verb)

5. We sell one-third of our products in our country and _____ (*no change*) the rest to other countries. (verb)

6. There is a big problem with our _____**tion**. The product isn't getting to the stores. (noun)

7. We need to _____ (*no change*) a new copy machine. (verb)

8. Our sales team received a higher _____ (*no change*) than we expected for our work in Alaska.

Discourse Markers: Sequencing

Study the following discourse markers. They include discourse markers from the mini-lecture you heard in Activity 6 and from the extended lecture you will hear in Activity 13.

As we know,	is known as	Second	In my talk today
The following are some common examples		I'd like to emphasize	
Let me put it another way	Moving on	Incidentally	Any questions

NOTE: For a complete list of discourse markers, see Appendix 6, page 140.

Sequencing with Discourse Markers

Sequencing means putting things in the right order.

- Read a teacher's notes on the similarities of business and marriage. The notes are not in the right order.
- Add numbers to show the correct order of the lecture.
- When you have finished, look at the discourse markers (**in bold type**). Choose similar discourse markers from the box on the previous page and write them above the phrases in bold.

The first one has been done for you.

☐ But **there's another way to say this**. Business is a basic human way of

relating, and **I think it is important to say** that the social relationship of marriage is like a business deal and is based on buying and selling.

☐ **By the way**, unsuccessful marriages, like unsuccessful business deals, often don't work because the partners can't agree on the "prices" for their behavior or are unwilling to sell them at any price.

In my talk today

1 **In today's lecture** I want discuss the question that many people ask:

"What is business?" **Everyone understands that** business is the activity of buying and selling things in order to earn money.

☐ Oh, . . . I see we are running out of time, so **going to a new subject**, we need to discuss the field trip to the Fly-By-Night Travel Agency next

Tuesday. You have the schedule. **Is there anything you want to ask me?**

☐ What deals do they have to make? **Let's look at some typical ones**. First, some men like to stay out late with their friends, but a new husband has to "sell" (in the sense of trading) that behavior to his wife in order to earn something greater from her—her care and affection.

☐ When people get married they make an agreement with each other.

"Making a contract" **is understood as** a business expression, but the newly married couple makes a contract too, and they have to make "deals" with each other to make that contract work.

☐ Third, they must make deals with each other about who is responsible for different things, like their budget and household responsibilities.

☐ **Next**, maybe the new wife likes to spend a lot of time with her parents, but the husband wants more time to be alone with her. So, she has to "sell" some of her time with her parents to him so that the relationship can work.

Regular Past Tense and Past Participles

In your studies of the English language, you have probably come across the rule of creating the past tense and past participles of regular verbs. In English, we add *-d* or *-ed* to regular verbs to make them past tense or to create the past participle.

> **talk/talk<u>ed</u>**

It is fairly simple to recognize and form the past tense in reading and writing. When it comes to listening and speaking, however, distinguishing the past tense might be a bit more difficult. Although forming the past tense of regular verbs simply requires the addition of *-d* or *-ed*, it can be challenging to hear this ending in spoken English.

The basic pronunciation of the regular past tense and participle ending of a verb is divided into three groups:

- [t] ending as in the verb *walked* [wôkt]
- [d] ending as in the verb *lived* [lĭvd]
- [ĭd] ending as in the verb *hated* [**hāt´** ĭd]

ACTIVITY

Listen for Past Forms

A. The following sentences, with the verbs underlined, are taken from the conversations and lectures in this chapter. As you listen to the sentences, circle the final sound you hear. The first one is done for you.

1. On Wednesday we <u>started</u> Chapter 6.   [t] [d] ([ĭd])

2. On Monday, we <u>looked</u> at the homework from the last class.   [t] [d] [ĭd]

3. I <u>missed</u> both classes on European labor regulations last week.   [t] [d] [ĭd]

4. International trade has <u>changed</u> because of improvements in technology.   [t] [d] [ĭd]

5. This <u>happened</u> for two reasons.   [t] [d] [ĭd]

6. when trains, automobiles, and planes were <u>invented</u>.   [t] [d] [ĭd]

7. With these improvements, business deals could be made more quickly and products could be <u>ordered</u> …   [t] [d] [ĭd]

8. and <u>distributed</u> *within* countries …   [t] [d] [ĭd]

9. and <u>exported</u> between countries in much less time.   [t] [d] [ĭd]

B. With a partner, practice reading the sentences you just heard. Try to exaggerate the final sound of the underlined verbs. Then compare your circled answers. Can you figure out the rules for pronouncing the endings [t], [d], and [ĭd]?

Vocabulary

Academic Word List

Practice reading and saying aloud these vocabulary words. How many do you already know?

1. **assess** [ə sĕs´] v. to analyze and determine the significance or value of something

   Managers must <u>assess</u> the skills of their employees.

2. **consume** [kən sōōm´] v. to use, eat, or drink up

   Some American cars <u>consume</u> a lot of gasoline.

3. **derive** [dĭ rīv´] v. to obtain or receive from a source

   Much of Turkmenistan's export finance is <u>derived</u> from the sale of oil and natural gas.

4. **economy** [ĭ kon´ ə mē] n. the economic (relating to the production, development, and management of wealth) system of a country, region, or state.

   Japan's <u>economy</u> is the second biggest in the world.

5. **estimate** [es´ tə māt´] v. to make a judgment about the approximate cost, quantity, or size or something. [ĕs´ tə mĭt] n. an approximate calculation

   The company <u>estimates</u> that its sales will increase by 12 percent. (v)
   I think the bank's <u>estimate</u> of my property's value is too low. (n)

6. **income** [ĭn´ kŭm] n. the amount of money received from work, the sale of property or goods, or from financial investments.

   Most people's <u>income</u> comes from their jobs.

7. **labor** [lā´ bər] adj. describing physical or mental effort or work. n. people who work for wages. v. to work

   A big <u>labor</u> sector of that country works mostly in the electronics industries. (adj)
   A <u>lot of labor</u> in this country is represented by organizations called unions. (n)
   Many workers <u>labor</u> in factories all day. (v.)

8. **policy** [pŏl´ ĭ sē] n. a plan, principle, or course of action

   The government <u>policy</u> on immigration may be changed next year.

9. **regulate** [rĕg´ yə lāt´] v. to control or direct something according to a rule or law

   The government <u>regulates</u> the food and drug industries.

10. **sector** [sĕk´ tər] or [sĕk´ tôr´] n. a division of something; a particular group of people or institutions in society defined by certain shared characteristics; e.g., the labor sector or the industrial sector

    The agricultural <u>sector</u> of the United States produces food that is sold all over the world.

Vocabulary Practice

Read the paragraph. Then complete the paragraph with words from the Academic Word List on the previous page. Some of the words may be in the plural or participle form.

The government's new _____ on the sale of meat has hurt the cattle and meat packing _____ of the food industry. Those hardest hit are small businesses, whose _____ will drop by 30 percent once the new rules go into effect. The large businesses _____ their income from a variety of sources and won't lose so much money, but small family businesses and workers depend entirely on this one source of income. The government says that it must _____ the industry more because of recent findings about tainted meat, and it has promised to _____ the damage that the new regulations will cause to businesses and the _____ sector. The government already _____ the costs to be in the 100s of millions of dollars, but it will not change the policy, despite its effect on the nation's _____, and has warned its citizens not to _____ any meat without the new inspection stamp until the situation is under control.

Listen and Respond

Listen and Use Strategies You Learned

First Listening: Listen for Vocabulary You will hear an extended lecture played two times. The first time, listen for words from the Academic Word List on page 55 and write them in the order you hear them.

1. _____
2. _____
3. _____
4. _____
5. _____

6. _____
7. _____
8. _____
9. _____
10. _____

Second Listening: Listen and Take Notes Listen to the extended lecture again. Take notes below using the word map outline method.

GLOBAL
ECONOMY
ISSUES

Now compare your notes with classmates. What information, if any, did you or they miss?

_____

_____

ACTIVITY 14 **Answer Questions about the Extended Lecture**

Find the answers to the following questions in your word map from Activity 13. Do not write the answers, just study them. Your teacher will tell you when to stop and put your notes away. Then write the answers to the questions from memory.

1. Name and describe three issues that are raised when a company moves its operations to a new country.

   _____

   _____

   _____

2. Describe the environmental issues that the global marketplace must solve in the twenty-first century.

   _____

   _____

   _____

SPEAKING **Extemporaneous Speaking**

Extemporaneous speaking means to speak without time to prepare your thoughts. Another way to say this is "to speak off the top of your head."

Give an Extemporaneous Speech

Task

You will give a two-minute extemporaneous reaction to a statement. Your teacher will give every student in the class a number. Then he or she will read a statement to react to (see suggestions at the end of the activity) and say a number. If your number is called, begin talking about the statement.

For example, your statement might be: "I think people should not have to stay after hours at work when their bosses ask them to."

You might begin your reaction with: "I agree. In my opinion, a person's private life is important. People need time with their families or just free time for themselves. If people don't have this private time then they may not do such a good job at work. For example, ..."

When you are finished, the teacher will call another number in the group. If that number is yours, you have two minutes to respond to what the first student said. Then your teacher will offer a different statement for the next round of responses.

Strategies for Extemporaneous Speaking

1. As you consider the statement, ask yourself if you agree or disagree and why.
2. Begin speaking by repeating the statement.
3. Introduce your thoughts with an introductory phrase. Here are some suggestions:

in my opinion	I believe	It's a tough question	I think that
I don't have personal experience with this, but ...			
I have firsthand experience with this			

4. Because there is a two-minute time limit, you need to get your ideas out quickly. Try to keep talking and let one thought lead to the next.
5. End with a summary or conclusion sentence of your ideas or opinions.

Possible Topics for Extemporaneous Speaking

1. Businesses should not move to other countries just so they can pay lower wages to the workers.
2. We need one international organization that controls multinational business.
3. I would rather have a female boss than a male boss.
4. There is too much government regulation in the business world.
5. Developed countries are not interested in the economies of developing countries.
6. No religious symbols or clothing should be allowed in the workplace.
7. If having a higher standard of living means we have a lot of pollution, then that's okay.
8. Men are naturally better at business than women.

NOTE: For more ideas, see *elt.thomson.com/keyconcepts.*

Ask Questions

Find at least two students who are interested in studying business. Ask them the following questions:

1. Why are you interested in business?

2. What aspect of business are you most interested in?

3. What type of business do you hope to enter?

4. What are your long-term goals in business?

 For more activities and information, go to the *Key Concepts 1* website at *elt.heinle.com/keyconcepts*.

4 • From the Social Sciences: American Government

POS 101
Introduction to American Government (3)

This course covers the structure and function of the American government and the forces involved in political change, placing particular emphasis on how the political system addresses and resolves important issues in modern American society.

An American government course is one of the choices available in community colleges and universities to fulfill social science requirements. This course can be of great value to you. A basic knowledge of the United States Constitution and the Bill of Rights will enable you to understand more about the U.S. political system and the differences between it and other forms of government.

Look at the description for an American Government course. Now find a course description for an introductory American government course from your community college or university catalog. What similarities do the two courses have? What are the differences?

This chapter will help you understand some **key concepts** about the establishment of the United States such as

- the reasons behind the United States' independence from England

- the creation and important principles of the United States Constitution

- the Bill of Rights and the important amendments that came after it

- some controversial issues in American society that relate to the Bill of Rights and the amendments

You will also practice some academic skills for success.

Get Ready To Listen

ACTIVITY **1**

Brainstorming and Discussion

Most people know that a citizen's duty is to obey the laws of the government. However, many people don't stop and think about the citizen–government relationship from the opposite point of view. Citizens of a country must follow the laws created by their government, but what rights should a government guarantee its citizens?

A. Make a list of rights that you believe every citizen should have in a society. *Suggestion:* Think of rights people may or may not have in the United States and other countries, for example, the right to medical care.

_____

_____

_____

_____

B. Get together in groups and compare your lists of rights. Did you have similar answers? Do you agree or disagree with your classmates? Explain your point of view to the others in your group.

C. Make a master list of all the rights your group members have listed and write it on the board. Your teacher may call on you to explain the reasons for your choices to the rest of the class.

Understand Phrasal Verbs Through Context

A phrasal verb is a combination of a verb and a preposition (particle) that makes a meaning that is usually different from the meaning of the verb alone. In spoken English, phrasal verbs are especially common. English speakers are more likely to ask "Could you **put out** your cigarette?" than "Could you **extinguish** your cigarette?"

The information below will help you understand the phrasal verbs used in the short conversations you will hear. Look at these two sentences:

> I want to **get** a new car. (The verb *get* means "obtain.")
> What time do you **get up**? (The phrasal verb *get up* means "get out of bed.")

Read the following conversation between two students.

> *Jorge:* Have you finished the paper the professor gave us to do last week in our English class? It's due tomorrow.
> *Samir:* To tell the truth, I have no idea what to do, so I have **put it off**. Could you explain it to me so that I can get started?

The phrasal verb **put off** may be one you haven't heard before, but if you understand the other words, you can figure it out. Samir says he is very confused and asks Jorge for help. Because the paper is due the next day and he hasn't started it, his answer suggests that to **put off** something means to avoid doing something a person needs to do. This is an example of understanding unfamiliar words by understanding the sentence or conversation (the context) they appear in.

Look at another example.

> *Sol:* Excuse me, Professor Jahelka, but I didn't understand your last comment.
> *Professor Jahelka:* I'm sorry, but could you please **hold off** asking questions? I'll answer any questions you have at the end of the lecture.

To figure out the meaning of **hold off**, consider that Professor Jahelka doesn't answer Sol's question. She says that she will answer all questions later, so you can conclude that **hold off** means "wait until a later time."

Usage Note

The object (noun) can occur after the phrasal verb, and, with many phrasal verbs, the object (a noun or pronoun) can occur between the two parts.

> You should *look up* **the word** in the dictionary.
> You should *look* **the word** *up* in the dictionary.
> You should *look* **it** *up* in the dictionary.

However, a pronoun can *never* come after a phrasal verb.

> *Wrong:* You should ~~look up it~~ in the dictionary.

Phrasal Verbs with More than One Meaning

Be careful! Some phrasal verbs can have two different meanings. Study these two examples:

I will **drop by** your house at noon.
(*Drop by* in this sentence means "to visit.")

I will **drop** the TV **by** your house at noon.
(*Drop ... by* in this example means "to deliver.")

Some Phrasal Verbs Indivisible

Some phrasal verbs, depending on their meaning, cannot be divided. When *drop by* means "to visit," you can't separate the phrase. Look what happens to the meaning of the sentence above if you put the object in the middle.

I will **drop** *your house* **by** at noon.

For a list of common phrasal verbs, see Appendix 7, page 142.

Listen and Respond

Listen for Phrasal Verbs

With a partner or a small group, listen to the campus conversations. Each conversation includes a phrasal verb. Choose from the list below and write the phrasal verbs you hear. Then circle the letter of the choice that best defines each phrasal verb.

keep up with	sit out	go over	filled up
figure out	nodding off	drop out	was up to me

Conversation 1: _____
    a. go farther   b. join
    c. talk longer than before   d. review or explain

Conversation 2: _____
    a. falling asleep   b. agreeing
    c. leaving   d. getting the wrong answer

Conversation 3: _____
    a. analyze   b. not fall behind
    c. memorize   d. organize

Conversation 4: _____
    a. my decision   b. her turn
    c. a bad choice   d. too late

Conversation 5: _____
    a. rest during   b. not participate in
    c. leave   d. not move during

Conversation 6: _____
    a. make a decision about   b. take notes on
    c. keep   d. change

Conversation 7: _____
    a. had too much   b. lost
    c. written in all the   d. studied
       available space

Conversation 8: _____
    a. stop attending   b. fail
    c. be late   d. pay

Vocabulary

Academic Word List

Practice reading and saying aloud these vocabulary words. How many of the words do you already know?

1. **authority** [ə thôr´ ĭ tē] [ə thŏr´ ĭ tē] n. the power to enforce laws, demand obedience, or judge

    The government has the <u>authority</u> to make rules for the country.

2. **concept** [kŏn´ sĕpt´] n. a general idea or understanding, especially one based on known facts or observation

    Freedom is a <u>concept</u> with different meanings to different people.

3. **establish** [ĭ stab´ lĭsh] v. to begin or set up something

    The country called the United States was <u>established</u> in the 1770s.

4. **impact** [ĭm´ păkt´] n. the effect of something. v. to have an effect on something

    The recent cuts in money for education have had a strong <u>impact</u> on the country's school system. (n)
    Rising fuel costs have <u>impacted</u> many people's car buying habits. (v)

5. **individual** [ĭn´ də vĭj´ o͞o əl] adj. relating to a single human, animal, plant, or thing. n. a single human, animal, plant, or thing

    The rights of the <u>individual</u> are guaranteed in our Constitution. (n)
    <u>Individual</u> values differ from one country to another. (adj)

6. **participate** [pär tĭs´ ə pāt´] v. to join with others in doing something; be involved

    Democracy doesn't work unless people <u>participate</u> in it.

7. **period** [pĭr´ ē əd] n. an interval of time with a specified length or characterized by certain conditions

    The <u>period</u> called the Cold War between the United States and the Soviet Union lasted about forty years.

8. **principle** [prĭn´ sə pəl] n. a basic or fundamental belief

    Our country's government is based on democratic <u>principles</u>.

9. **restrict** [rĭ strĭkt´] v. to keep or confine somebody or something within limits

    The city government made a law that <u>restricts</u> where people can smoke in public places.

10. **role** [rōl] n. the characteristic or expected social behavior of a person, group, or organization

    The <u>roles</u> of husbands and wives in society have changed since my grandparents' time.

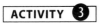

Vocabulary Practice

Complete each sentence with an Academic Word List word from the box. You may have to change the form of the word from singular to plural.

participate	establish	impact	restrict	concept
individual	period	role	principle	authority

1. The _____ of a president is to lead the country.

2. Average people have a right in democracies to _____ in political decisions.

3. A government _____ rules and laws for society.

4. A president in the U.S. is elected to serve for a _____ of four years.

5. Democracy is based on the idea that the _____ is as important as the group.

6. A _____ of law in democracies is that people are innocent until they are proven guilty.

7. A judge has the _____ to send criminals to prison.

8. The new health-care law will have a strong _____ on how people receive medical treatment.

9. The U.S. Constitution says that the government cannot _____ people's right to say what they think.

10. People have many different _____ about what a government should do for its citizens.

Taking Notes: The Cornell Method

Many students use the Cornell method to take notes. In this method you divide the paper into two columns. You record main points in the left column and related or supporting details in the right column. One advantage of this system is that you can return later to the notes and add comments to help you organize the information better. For example, you can add question words such as *who* or *where* if the information answers those questions.

ACTIVITY 4   *Practice the Cornell Method*

Read the following paragraph. Then complete the chart below using the Cornell method of note taking.

European people lived in America long before the government of the United States was formed. When the Pilgrims, the first organized group of settlers, came over from England in 1620 on the ship called the Mayflower, European fishermen had already come before them and mingled with the Native Americans. One of these Native Americans was named Samoset. Samoset knew some English because of his association with English fishermen. He introduced the settlers to the chief of his tribe, the Massasoit. We get the state name Massachusetts from the name of this Native American tribe. The Pilgrims and the Massasoit chief gave each other gifts and signed a Treaty of Friendship. The Massasoit helped the Pilgrims learn how to fish, hunt, and farm. This friendship helped the Pilgrims survive through the first difficult years in their new homeland.

MAIN POINTS	SUPPORTING DETAILS
Europeans in America before it was U.S.	• Pilgrims, _____ settlers • ship _____, 1620 • European _____ before P. • _____ American • knew _____ • introduced P. to chief of Massasoit tribe
Treaty of Friendship	• taught P. to _____, _____, _____ • helped P. _____

Listen and Respond

ACTIVITY **5**

Listen and Use Strategies You Learned

First Listening: Listen for Vocabulary You will hear a mini-lecture played two times. The first time, listen for vocabulary from the Academic Word List on page 66. Put a number in the blank next to each word as you hear it. Number 1 has been done for you.

_**1**_ period	_____ established	_____ impact	_____ concept
_____ role	_____ restrict	_____ authority	_____ participate
_____ principles	_____ individual		

Second Listening: Listen and Take Notes Listen to the mini-lecture again. In the space provided, try the Cornell method of note taking.

MAIN POINTS	SUPPORTING DETAILS
U.S. formed in eighteenth century	• period of political change in Europe • •
new country after war of independence	•
2 guiding principles of U.S. constitution	• •

Answer Comprehension Questions about the Mini-Lecture

Use your notes in Activity 5 to answer these questions about the mini-lecture. Circle the letter of the best answer.

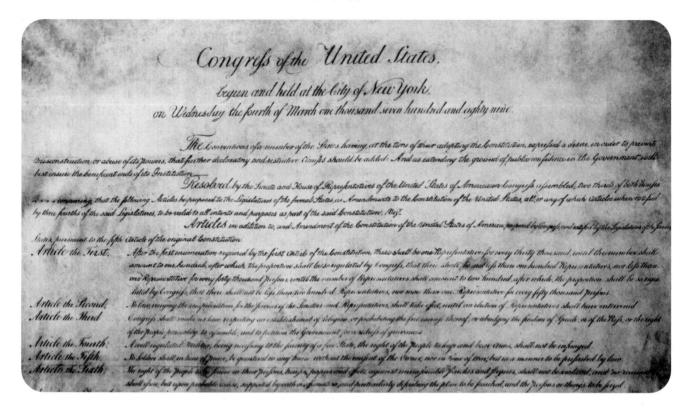

1. Who were the people of Europe struggling against?
   a. the U.S.
   b. the colonies
   c. royalty

2. When was the Constitution of the United States established?
   a. in 1876
   b. during the late 1700s
   c. in the early eighteenth century

3. Who designed the Constitution?
   a. all the people living in the colonies
   b. England
   c. landowners and intellectuals in the colonies

4. Which two concepts are principles of the Constitution?
   a. individualism and democracy
   b. government restrictions and participation
   c. the power of authority and the rights of the individual

5. Which concept below can you infer *would not* fit with the American principles mentioned in the mini-lecture?
   a. the rights of the group are more important than the rights of the individual
   b. democracy depends on people being able to say what they think
   c. there should be no royalty in American society

Reduced ə Sound

Every word of more than one syllable in the English language has stress, where one syllable is more prominent than the others. In many words, especially those with more than two syllables, vowel sounds are reduced. Reduced sounds do not sound like the vowels that are written in the word. The reduced ə sound is similar to the *uh* sound you might make if you are punched in the stomach. Here is an example:

elephant

The word elephant contains two vowels, *e* and *a*. However, only the first vowel is pronounced as it is written, with the short *e* sound. The second and third vowels are reduced to what is called the schwa (symbolized as [ə]) .

The standard pronunciation of the word *elephant* is [ĕl′ ə fənt]

Listen for Vowel Reductions

A. You will hear the eight phrases below, which have been taken from the lectures in this chapter. Circle the words you hear that contain vowel reductions. There may be more than one circled word per phrase. Underline the reduced vowels. The first one is done for you.

1. this was in the eighteenth (cent<u>u</u>ry)

2. a big period of political change

3. after a successful war of independence from England

4. before I go into this crucial element

5. of our political system

6. something that would define and protect

7. to achieve more freedom for the individual

8. the rights of all citizens as well

B. Now compare your answers with a partner. Did you circle the same words and underline the same vowels? Practice saying the words and phrases aloud. Pay attention to the reduced vowels. How are their sounds different from the regular sounds of the vowels?

Vocabulary

Academic Word List

Practice reading and saying aloud these vocabulary words. How many of the words do you already know?

1. **achieve** [ə chēv´] v. to succeed in completing, producing, or gaining something

   Her goal was to <u>achieve</u> fame at the Olympics.

2. **administrate** [ăd mĭn´ ĭ strāt´] v. to manage or direct the affairs of something

   He <u>administrates</u> the state's health-care programs.

3. **design** [dĭ zīn´] v. to draw up plans, sketches, or drawings for something. n. a plan, drawing, or sketch, especially a detailed plan showing how something is to be made

   The citizen's action group wants the government to <u>design</u> a better transportation system. (v)
   I don't like the <u>design</u> of this year's new cars. (n)

4. **element** [ĕl´ ə mənt] n. a part of a whole, especially a fundamental or essential part

   An important <u>element</u> for success in politics is to listen to what the people want.

5. **institute** [ĭn´ stĭ tōot] v. to establish, organize, or set something in operation

   The city government <u>instituted</u> a no-smoking rule in its offices.

6. **interpret** [ĭn tûr´ prĭt] v. to explain the meaning of or understand something in one's own way

   The United States courts <u>interpret</u> the country's laws.

7. **legal** [lē´ gəl] adj. permitted by law

   A passport is a <u>legal</u> document that a person needs for travel in other countries.

8. **legislate** [lĕj´ ĭ slāt´] v. to make or pass laws

   The government in Washington, D.C. <u>legislates</u> the laws for the United States.

9. **region** [rē´ jən] n. a large area of the earth, space, or the body

   Many Mexican-Americans live in the Southwest <u>region</u> of the United States.

10. **seek** [sēk] v. to search for or to try to locate something

    Because of the oil shortage, people are <u>seeking</u> alternative forms of energy.

Vocabulary Practice

Complete each sentence with an Academic Word List word from the box. You may have to change the ending of the word.

legal	legislate	interpret	achieve	institute
element	administrate	region	design	seek

1. The finance minister resigned his position because after six years he didn't want to _____ such a big program anymore.

2. Professor Shettle, could you please _____ this law we're studying? I don't understand it.

3. The government _____ a new law that changes the rule for exporting products.

4. The politician _____ a new program that provided parents with more time off from work right after their children are born, but it hasn't been approved yet.

5. That citizens' group _____ to change the laws on tobacco.

6. The various _____ of America have different political attitudes. For example, the South is generally more conservative than the North.

7. The rights of the individual are an important _____ of the U.S. Constitution.

8. Every year the university _____ new policies regarding registration and tuition.

9. Twenty-one is the _____ age for drinking alcohol in my country.

10. In order to _____ her goal of finishing law school, Leslie practically lives at the library.

Listen and Respond

Listen and Use Strategies You Learned

First Listening: Listen for Vocabulary You will hear an extended lecture played two times. The first time, listen for words from the academic word list. Circle the exact words you hear.

1.	elements	element
2.	designed	design
3.	instituted	institute
4.	regions	region
5.	legislative	legislate
6.	administer	administrate
7.	interpret	interpreted
8.	achieved	achieve
9.	legal	legalized
10.	seeks	seek

Second Listening: Listen and Take Notes Listen to the extended lecture again. Use the Cornell Method to take notes about what you hear in the spaces provided below and on the next page.

TOPIC: BILL OF RIGHTS	
_____ branches of government	
_____ Founding Fathers	
Bill of Rights	

TOPIC: BILL OF RIGHTS	
problems with original Amendments	
avoided slavery	
Slow change	
Crucial point of Constitution	

Now, in small groups, compare your notes. Does the information you recorded differ from your classmates' information? If so, think of some reasons why the notes are different. As a group, decide which notes are important and which are not important. Write the most important information in the space below.

Answer Comprehension Questions about the Extended Lecture

Circle the letter of the correct answer to each question. You can use your notes from Activity 9.

1. Which branch of the U.S. government decides if a law is constitutional?
   a. the judicial branch
   b. the executive branch
   c. the legislative branch
   d. the presidential branch

2. Which of the following is true?
   a. There are ten amendments to the U.S. Constitution.
   b. The first amendment to the U.S. Constitution was written in 1920.
   c. There are at least 19 amendments in the U.S. Constitution.
   d. The U.S. Constitution can no longer be amended.

3. What was an important issue not covered in the constitution that caused conflict later?
   a. slavery
   b. the right to bear arms
   c. the thirteenth amendment
   d. the right to religious expression

4. Who got the right to vote first?
   a. British immigrants
   b. white men
   c. African Americans
   d. women

5. What is a good title for this lecture?
   a. How the U.S. Government Works
   b. Current Rights in the United States
   c. The Right to Vote
   d. The Constitution and the Rights of the People

Think Critically: What Do You Remember?

A. David has written a paper on how the government functions. He has it all wrong! You're his teacher. Without looking at your notes, put a line through his errors and write the correct information above them. The first error is corrected for you. There are ten more.

                                       three

The U.S. government is divided into ~~four~~ branches. The executive branch makes the laws, the legislative branch approves them, and the judicial branch administrates them. At the end of the U.S. Constitution there were eight original amendments.

Other amendments, made earlier, guarantee the president more individual rights. One of these amendments institutes slavery. It was made before the Civil War. Another one gives children the right to vote. The Constitution is a very important document and it cannot be changed.

B. Now look at your notes from the extended lecture in Activity 9. In the box below, write down the information you missed. As you can see, good note taking is an important part of being a good student.

Discourse Markers: Transitions

ACTIVITY 12 *Define Transition Signals*

The discourse markers in the left column below signal transitions in information, as most discourse markers do. All these discourse markers were used in the extended lecture you heard. What do you think they mean? Match them with the definitions on the left. You may want to listen to the lecture again. The first one is done for you.

1. My topic today …
2. It is understood …
3. Let me give you some specific examples.
4. The crucial point is …
5. It follows then …
6. i.e.,
7. All right
8. Let's now look at …
9. as well
10. in short

_____ so

_____ also

_____ okay

__1__ today we're going to talk about

_____ at this time let's examine

_____ we already know

_____ this point is the most important

_____ Here are some of the things I'm talking about.

_____ in other words

_____ to summarize

NOTE: For a complete list of *Key Concepts 1* discourse markers and their functions, see Appendix 6, page 140.

SPEAKING • Debating

ACTIVITY 13 *Participate in a Debate*

In this activity, you and your classmates will participate in an informal debate for or against the Constitutional Amendments. A debate is a forum where people with opposing points of view discuss and argue their opinions for and against an issue. A debate usually ends with one side being chosen as the winner. Here is one procedure for debate.

Strategies for Debate

Do the following for each of the four controversies:

1. Choose a controversy.
2. Choose one person in the class to serve as the mediator of the debate. A mediator's job is to maintain order and to make sure that the groups are following the time limits.
3. Get together in a group that shares the same opinion (*for* or *against*) on an issue. This is your debate team.

4. Compare your answers with the other members of your debate team. On a separate sheet of paper, make a list of the three best points that support your argument.
5. Choose one member to present the group's opinions and supporting points. Each group will have three minutes for this presentation.
6. While you listen to the group that has the opposing opinion, take notes about what they say. Each group will be given two minutes to organize a *rebuttal* (reply to the other group's points) when they are finished.
7. Choose a different person from your group to give a two-minute rebuttal.
8. Open the discussion to anyone in either group to respond again to the arguments of the opposing group.

Sample Debate Sequence

Group 1: YES (three-minute limit)

A. Introduce the topic and opinion

> **Religious expression SHOULD be allowed in public schools.**

B. Give supporting reasons for opinion

> **"There are many reasons, but the main ones are …"**

C. Give a concluding statement

> **"We urge you to support our position because …"**

Group 2: NO (three-minute limit)

A. Give opinions and supporting reasons
B. Give a concluding statement

Group 1:

A. Organize rebuttal privately (two-minute limit)
B. Present rebuttal (two-minute limit)

> **"We respectfully disagree with Group 2's opinion that …"**

C. Offer reasons why Group 2's ideas are wrong

> **"Group 2's ideas are illogical because … "**

Group 2:

A. Organize rebuttal privately (two-minute limit)
B. Present rebuttal (two-minute limit)

Groups 1 and 2 (five-minute limit):

The floor is open to individuals from both groups to give their opinions.

Mediator (two-minute limit):

Make a decision and declare the winner of the debate.

Background

In the extended lecture, you learned that amendments are changes to laws or added laws. It is important to remember that just because an amendment has been added to the constitution does *not* mean that everyone agrees with it. For instance, the first and second amendments in the Bill of Rights have been debated continuously throughout the history of the United States. Sometimes these laws are challenged all the way to the Supreme Court—the highest court in the country. The Supreme Court then decides whether the law is indeed constitutional or whether it needs to be changed or eliminated. Let's look at these two amendments and examine why they have created so much controversy.

> Amendment I: "Congress shall make no law respecting (about) the establishment of religion, or prohibiting the free expression thereof, or abridging the freedom of speech, or of the press, or the right of the people to peaceably assemble, and to petition the Government for a redress of grievances."

> CONTROVERSY #1: "… no law respecting the establishment of religion …"

These words have been interpreted by the Supreme Court to mean that religion and government should be completely separate and there should be no religious activities officially connected with any government activity or institution.

Over the years there have been schools, which are funded by the federal and state governments, that have instituted a prayer time in the classroom at the beginning of each school day. People opposed to the prayers say that this violates the separation of religion and government stated in the First Amendment.

Question for debate: *Should any religious expression be allowed in public schools?*

> CONTROVERSY #2: "… no law … abridging (reducing) the freedom of speech, or the press (media) …"

These words have been interpreted by the Supreme Court to mean that people and the media have a right to say or print whatever they want and the government can't stop them.

This amendment was designed by our founders to allow citizens to criticize the government. However, because this amendment includes *all* speech, pornography and violent material can easily be seen by children on the Internet.

Question for debate: *Should there be some limits on free speech?*

These words mean that people have the right to demonstrate publicly about anything that they have an opinion about.

In 1989, the American flag was burned in a demonstration. The flag is a powerful symbol for Americans. It is the subject of the national anthem. A famous statue depicts American soldiers raising the flag after a particularly hard-won battle in World War II in which many Americans were killed. When the flag was burned, many Americans were outraged. Texas passed a law making flag burning illegal, but the Supreme Court found the law unconstitutional. The Court stated that flag burning is free expression protected by the Constitution. What do you think?

Question for debate: *Should people have the right to burn **their country's** flag in public?*

Star Spangled Banner

Oh, say can you see, by the dawn's early light,
What so proudly we hailed at the twilight's last gleaming?
Whose broad stripes and bright stars, through the perilous fight,
O'er the ramparts we watched, were so gallantly streaming?
And the rockets' red glare, the bombs bursting in air,
Gave proof through the night that our flag was still there.
O say, does that star-spangled banner yet wave
O'er the land of the free and the home of the brave?

Amendment II: "A well regulated militia, being necessary to the security of a free State, the right of the people to keep and bear Arms (weapons) shall not be infringed (restricted)."

> CONTROVERSY #4: "… the right of the people to keep and bear Arms …"

America has the highest rate of gun violence in the industrialized world. Many Americans own handguns for self-protection. However, these guns more often accidentally kill family members (often children who are playing with them) than people trying to harm the gun owners.

All kinds of guns can be bought by U.S. citizens.

Question for debate: *Should the right to own a gun be absolute, i.e., without any limits?*

Task

Answer the questions below that address each controversy. Circle your opinion—*yes* or *no*—and write the reasons for your opinion.

1. Should any religious expression be allowed in public schools?   YES   NO

_____

_____

_____

_____

2. Should there be some limits on free speech?   YES   NO

_____

_____

_____

_____

3. Should people have the right to burn their country's flag in public?   YES   NO

_____

_____

_____

_____

4. Should the right to own a gun be absolute, i.e., without any limits?   YES   NO

_____

_____

_____

_____

Find Out about More Key Concepts

Find an American government teacher or a student who is currently studying government. Question this person about what he or she considers a **key concept** in the field of American government. Take notes and share your findings with the class.

 For more activities and information, go to the *Key Concepts 1* website at *elt.heinle.com/keyconcepts*.

Charles Darwin (1809 – 1882)
British naturalist who contributed to the study of evolution

**BIO 101
Introduction to
Biological Science**

The topics studied in an introductory biology class have an impact on how we understand everyday life. Understanding the basics of biology is key to comprehending life in general. It encompasses the study of the basic history of life on Earth, the organisms that share our planet with us, the evolution and reproduction of organisms, and many other topics.

5 • From the Biological Sciences: • Biology

Biology is the study of all forms of life, from the smallest microorganisms to entire ecosystems. Most colleges and universities require their students to take at least two courses in the natural sciences, with biology being among the most popular. Read the above description of a biology course.

Now find a course description for an introductory biology course from your community college or university catalog. What similarities do the two courses have? What are the differences?

This chapter will help you understand some **key concepts** of biology, such as

- how organisms evolve or change over time

- factors that determine your survival in everyday life

- the connection between organisms and their environment

- factors that could lead to the extinction of a group of organisms

You will also practice some academic skills for success.

Get Ready to Listen

ACTIVITY ❶

Brainstorming and Discussion

Look at the illustration and answer the questions.

The Importance of Biology

1. Study the cartoon. Write a description of what you see.

   _____

   _____

2. How are the shorter people trying to get some apples?

   _____

   _____

3. Imagine that the only way that all the people in the cartoon can eat the apples is by picking them by themselves. Does this sound improbable? Based on the picture, who is the person most likely to survive in this strange place?

   _____

   _____

4. Now imagine this same population 1,000 years from now. If this population has survived, what changes must these people have gone through? In other words, how will they have adapted to their environment?

   _____

   _____

Congratulations! You have just formulated a **natural selection** hypothesis.

Listen and Respond

ACTIVITY 2

Listen for Phrasal Verbs in Context

With a partner or a small group, listen to the conversations. Each conversation includes a phrasal verb. Choose from the list below and write the phrasal verbs you hear. Then circle the letter of the sentence that best answers the question.

look over	put … off	hand in	getting over
pass out	make … up	give up	ran out of

Conversation 1: Phrasal verb: <u>getting over</u>

1. Why didn't Bill go to the library?
   - a. Bill was buying something.
   - b. Bill was recovering from a sickness.
   - c. Bill was climbing a mountain.
   - d. Bill was making his bed.

Conversation 2: Phrasal verb: _____

2. What does the teacher want?
   - a. to congratulate the students on their hard work
   - b. to give some biology notes to the students
   - c. to hand-write some notes
   - d. to collect the biology notes

Conversation 3: Phrasal verb: _____

3. What does the student ask Professor Jones to do?
   - a. to review her answer
   - b. to help her find the answer
   - c. to answer the question for her
   - d. to do some research on question number 3.

Conversation 4: Phrasal verb: _____

4. What does the professor mean?
   - a. He does not believe the student.
   - b. Students cannot do the experiment on another day.
   - c. Students can do the experiment on another day, but they will receive a lower score.
   - d. Students can write an inventive essay in place of the lab experiment.

Conversation 5: Phrasal verb: _____

5. What did Shelly do?
   - a. She lost her research paper.
   - b. She put her research paper away.
   - c. She began writing it too late.
   - d. She did not begin writing her research paper.

Conversation 6: Phrasal verb: _____

6. What happened to the student who was dissecting the frog?
   a. She got lost.
   b. Her watch broke.
   c. She didn't finish.
   d. She didn't understand the last two questions.

Conversation 7: Phrasal verb: _____

7. What is Josh going to do?
   a. leave the classroom
   b. distribute some papers to the students
   c. report some information to the class
   d. collect papers from the students

Conversation 8: Phrasal verb: _____

8. What will Anna do?
   a. help someone else
   b. give her notes to the teacher
   c. ask for help
   d. stop trying

Vocabulary

Academic Word List

Practice reading and saying aloud these vocabulary words. How many of the words do you already know?

1. **acquire** [ə kwīr´] v. to gain possession of (something); to get (something) by one's own efforts

   Only a few animals have <u>acquired</u> the ability to survive in an extremely harsh environment.

2. **aspect** [ăs´ pĕkt] n. feature; a way in which something can be considered

   The one <u>aspect</u> of biology that I really don't like is all the memorization I have to do.

3. **assist** [ə sĭst´] v. to help or aid. n. an act of giving help or aid

   My tutor has <u>assisted</u> me in learning about cell functions. (v)
   My lab partner gave me a quick <u>assist</u> with my experiment. (n)

4. **conclude** [kən klōōd´] v. to form an opinion about something; to finish

   The staff meeting <u>concluded</u> on a bad note because the head of the science department got into an argument with the academic affairs dean.

5. **environment** [ĕn vī´ rən mənt] *or* [ĕn vī´ ərn mənt] n. all of the surroundings and conditions that affect the growth and development of living things; the social and cultural conditions affecting the nature of a person or community

   The natural <u>environment</u> for penguins is the Antarctic.

6. **factor** (in) [făk´ tər] n. something that helps cause a certain result; an element or ingredient. v. to consider

   Many <u>factors</u> lead to the extinction of a particular species. (n)
   When you study animal behavior, you have to <u>factor</u> in the animal's environment. (v)

7. **feature** [fē´ chər] n. a prominent part or characteristic. v. to give special attention to something or someone

   A special <u>feature</u> of humans is their ability to speak. (n)
   Next week's lecture will <u>feature</u> some researchers from Smith-Clark laboratories. (v)

8. **function** [fŭngk´ shən] n. a purpose; an assigned duty or activity. v. to work; to operate

   I still don't understand what the <u>function</u> of the kidney is. (n)
   Dr. Jones is a full professor here, but he also <u>functions</u> as the chair of the biology department. (v)

9. **indicate** [ĭn´ dĭ kāt´] v. to show or point something out; to serve as a sign or symptom of something

   Strong genes <u>indicate</u> a good chance of survival.

10. **primary** [prī´ mĕr´ ē] *or* [prī´ mə rē] adj. first in importance, rank, or quality; original; basic

    The <u>primary</u> goal of this textbook is to help students understand academic concepts.

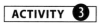

Vocabulary Practice

For each category labeled by a word from the Academic Word List, provide at least two other examples of the category.

1. different natural **environments**

   a forest _____   _a beach_ _____

   _____   _____

2. **functions** of modern inventions

   a car → for driving ___   _refrigerator →_ _____

   calculator → _____   _____ _→_ _____

3. **factors** that make you late for work

   waking up late _____   _____

   _____   _____

4. things you **acquire**

   a loan from the bank ___   _____

   _____   _____

5. things you **conclude**

   an essay or a speech ___   _____

   _____   _____

6. special **features** of a new car

   a car alarm _____   _____

   _____   _____

7. **aspects** of learning a foreign language

   the pronunciation _____   _____

   _____   _____

8. signs that **indicate** rules of the road

   a speed limit sign _____   _____

   _____   _____

9. things that **assist** you in studying

   a dictionary _____   _____

   _____   _____

10. **primary** goals of this textbook

    note-taking methods ___   _____

    _____   _____

Taking Notes: Key Words

Use Key Words

When you listen to a lecture, there will always be important vocabulary that you need to recognize and understand. Key words or phrases contain the essence of communication. They include specific *content words* (technical words that are related to the subject), names, numbers, equations, and words of degree, such as *better*, *most*, and *least*. Sometimes you can take effective notes just by writing down key words, transitions, or symbols to show the relationships between the words.

Study the example of the key word method below. The words in capital letters are key words that can help you remember specific content from the lecture.

DARWIN — developed theory of natural selection
HEREDITY — passed from one generation to the next
SURVIVAL — means offspring are produced

Special Vocabulary to Know

Studying these key words will help you as you listen to the mini-lecture.

genetic [jə nĕt´ ĭk] adj. relating to genes or genetics

> Some people with high cholesterol levels have <u>genetic</u> markers that make them more susceptible to this illness.

inherit (ed) [ĭn hĕr´ ĭt] v. (past participle) acquired by genetic transmission from one's parents or ancestors

(**NOTE:** The word *inherited* is often used as an adjective.)

> People <u>inherit</u> the color of their hair from their parents.

offspring [ôf´ sprĭng´] *or* [ŏf´ sprĭng´] n. the young or descendants of a person, an animal, or a plant

> A spider can produce thousands of <u>offspring</u> in its lifetime.

radical [răd´ ĭ kəl] adj. extreme

> Darwin's ideas about the origins of certain species were considered <u>radical</u> when they were first introduced.

species [spē´ shēz] *or* [spē´ sēz] n. a classification of similar animals or plants

> Which <u>species</u> of mammal do you think is the most docile?

trait [trāt] n. a distinctive feature

> Brothers and sisters often have different personality <u>traits</u>.

variable [vâr´ ē ə bəl] *or* [văr´ ē ə bəl] adj. changeable

> Fraternal twins have fewer <u>variable</u> genes than other brothers and sisters.

Listen and Respond

Listen and Use Strategies You Learned

First Listening: Listen for Discourse Markers You will hear a mini-lecture played two times. The first time, listen for the discourse markers. Fill in the blanks with the markers you hear. Their functions appear in parentheses under the blanks.

1. Good afternoon. _____ today is …
   (introducing)

2. First _____ that in the …
   (emphasizing)

3. _____, the process of …
   (clarifying)

4. _____ is condition number …
   (shifting subtopics)

5. _____, I want to mention …
   (digressing)

6. In biology, _____ the theory …
   (concluding)

Second Listening: Listen and Take Notes with Key Words Listen to the mini-lecture again. Take notes in the box below. Keep your notes as basic as possible and write down only key words.

Classify Words You Hear: Check Your Notes

Words are often classified into two categories: content words and function words. Content words have definite meanings. They are easy to define, such as *aspect*, *factor*, and *indicate*. Function words are usually smaller words that are difficult to define, such as *the* and *on*.

Review your notes. How many key words did you write in the box? If you wrote between 20 and 40 words, you probably got enough information from the lecture. If you wrote more than 50 words, examine the vocabulary. Did you write words that are not content words? That is, are they words with little meaning? Remember that a lot of time can be saved during the note-taking process by writing down only the key words.

ACTIVITY **5**

Check Information about the Mini-Lecture

Read the following statements about the mini-lecture. Circle *True* if the statement is correct and *False* if it is not. If the statement is false, change it to make it true. Refer to your notes to help you.

1. True / (False)   Charles Darwin developed the theory of ~~native~~ *natural* selection.

2. True / False   There are three conditions to Darwin's theory.

3. True / False   Individuals have different characteristics.

4. True / False   Darwin's second condition in natural selection states that certain traits help species survive better than others.

5. True / False   The environment is responsible for passing on certain characteristics.

6. True / False   According to the lecture, natural selection occurs with all life forms.

7. True / False   Biologists have not been able to replicate Darwin's study.

With a partner, compare your answers. For the answers you marked *False*, did you and your partner make the same changes to make the statements true?

Pronouncing Word Combinations in Sound Groups

When people speak naturally, they don't pronounce each word in isolation as if they were reciting a list:

The – teacher – gave – us – a – study – guide – for – next – week's – test.

Instead, they generally combine individual words into sound groups, often with subtle pauses between the groups:

The teacher / gave us / a study guide / for next week's test.

ACTIVITY **6**

Identify Sound Groups

Listen to the following sentences. Listen for subtle pauses and sound groups. Place slashes (/) between phrases to separate them into sound groups. The first one has been done for you.

1. First / we should bear in mind / that in the 1800s, / Darwin's ideas / were considered radical.

2. Now, there are three aspects of Darwin's theory.

3. That is to say, the process of natural selection occurs when three conditions are met.

4. The first condition is that individuals within a population have different characteristics.

5. The next point I'd like to focus on is condition number two.

6. This factor has to do with heredity.

7. Darwin noted that variable traits are *heritable*, meaning that they are passed on from one generation to the next.

8. One of the primary functions of all species is to survive and reproduce.

9. When a species does reproduce, it passes on genetic features from generation to generation.

Vocabulary

Academic Word List

Practice reading and saying aloud these vocabulary words. How many of the words do you already know?

1. **affect** [ə fĕkt´] v. to have an influence on; to bring about a change in something or someone

   My absences have <u>affected</u> my overall grade in the class.

2. **conduct** [kən dŭkt´] v. to direct the course of something; manage stress. [kŏn´ dŭkt´] n. the way a person acts

   Biologists have <u>conducted</u> many experiments in the Amazon Rain Forest. (v)
   My child's <u>conduct</u> last night at dinner was horrible. (n)

   NOTE: As a noun, the stress is on the first syllable.

3. **construct** [kən strŭkt´] v. to build or put together

   The city planners want to <u>construct</u> a high-speed train service, but environmentalists are protesting the plan.

4. **equate** [ĭ kwāt´] v. to make or consider something the same or equivalent

   Most people in the world <u>equate</u> Darwin with the idea of "survival of the fittest."

5. **focus** [fō´ kəs] n. center of interest, attention, or activity; emphasis. v. to concentrate; to adjust

   The <u>focus</u> of the experiment was to see the effects of heat on plant life. (n)
   Darwin <u>focused</u> his research on bird species of the Galapagos Islands. (v)

6. **injure** [ĭn´ jər] v. to hurt; to cause physical or emotional harm

   I <u>injured</u> my back during the football game.

7. **positive** [pŏz´ ĭ tĭv] adj. showing certainty or acceptance; absolutely certain. n. an affirmative element or characteristic

   Jim's studying certainly yielded <u>positive</u> results. He passed the test! (adj)
   The <u>positives</u> of building the new lab in the science center certainly outweigh the negatives. Student enrollment should increase this year. (n)

8. **range** [rānj] n. the extent of something; an amount of difference. v. to vary or move between specified limits

   The <u>range</u> of our assigned tasks in biology class is great. (n)
   The final exam grades <u>ranged</u> from scores of fifteen to ninety-three. (v)

9. **relevant** [rĕl´ ə vənt] adj. related to the matter being considered; pertinent

   Your question during the lecture yesterday wasn't <u>relevant</u> to the teacher's topic.

10. **strategy** [străt´ ə jē] n. a plan of action

    We need a unique <u>strategy</u> if we're going to win the science fair competition.

Vocabulary Practice

Circle the letter of the word that best completes each sentence.

1. That movie was so disturbing that it _____ my sleep last night.
   a. constructed   b. injured   c. affected   d. focused

2. If you don't _____ "final exam" with "study hard," you might fail the exam.
   a. equate   b. conduct   c. focus   d. range

3. Darwin _____ his theory of natural selection after many years of research.
   a. assisted   b. constructed   c. affected   d. injured

4. We didn't understand the main _____ of last week's lecture.
   a. focus   b. environment   c. conduct   d. range

5. You don't need to write that information down. It's not _____.
   a. focused   b. relevant   c. positive   d. constructed

6. It's important to note that an animal's _____ depends a lot on its environment.
   a. range   b. factor   c. conduct   d. aspect

7. Our professor canceled today's classes because she _____ her back over the weekend.
   a. assisted   b. injured   c. indicated   d. ranged

8. We were so happy that the teacher gave all of us _____ feedback on our research papers.
   a. acquired   b. primary   c. ranging   d. positive

9. My _____ of studying all night for the human biology final exam didn't work; I fell asleep during the test.
   a. strategy   b. range   c. aspect   d. function

10. Our test scores _____ from 28% to 92%.
    a. equated   b. ranged   c. focused   d. affected

Discourse Markers: More Transition Signals

Study the following phrases that signal transitions. You will hear many of these phrases used as discourse markers in the extended lecture.

Function	Phrase
To give background information	As we have all read
To list	Finally,
To show a connection	in connection with
To give examples	For example,
	Take X, for instance.
To set parameters	In the scope of

NOTE: For a complete list of discourse markers, see Appendix 6, page 140.

Special Vocabulary to Know

Studying these key words will help you as you listen to the extended lecture.

adapt [ə dăpt´] v. to change or adjust for a certain purpose

> **We had to adapt our eating habits when we went camping last year.**

ancestor [ăn´ sĕs´ tər] n. a person from whom one is descended

> **Women members of the group *Daughters of the American Revolution* have ancestors who lived in the United States in the late 1700s.**

finch [fĭnch] n. any of various songbirds with a short thick bill used for cracking seeds

> **There are many species of finches found on the Galapagos Islands.**

Listen and Respond

Listen and Use Strategies You Learned

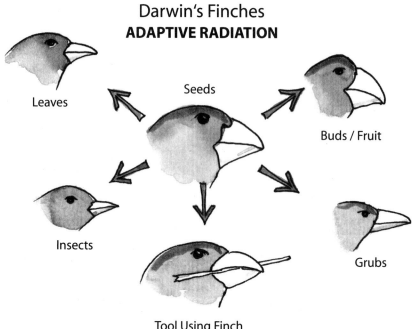

Darwin's Finches
ADAPTIVE RADIATION

Leaves

Seeds

Buds / Fruit

Insects

Grubs

Tool Using Finch

First Listening: Listen for Discourse Markers You will hear an extended lecture played two times. The first time, listen for discourse markers that organize the information. Put a check mark next to the words or phrases you hear.

1. _____ As we know,   _____ As we have all read,

2. _____ In the scope of   _____ In other words,

3. _____ Take the island finches,   _____ Take the island finches,
   for example.   for instance.

4. _____ First,   _____ For example,

5. _____ in connection with   _____ in common with

6. _____ Finally,   _____ Furthermore,

Second Listening: Listen and Take Notes with Key Words Listen to the extended lecture again. Take notes in the space provided. Use the key word method that you learned about on page 91 and write the most important information.

Write without Notes

Below is a list of important points from the lecture on Darwin and the Galapagos Islands. Write as much information as you can remember on each topic. Then check your notes to compare your answers.

1. Galapagos Islands _____

    _____

2. finches _____

    _____

3. beaks _____

    _____

4. natural selection _____

    _____

5. importance of Darwin's research _____

    _____

ACTIVITY **10**

Think Critically

Study the graphic representation of Darwin's theory of adaptive radiation. In your own words, describe the theory. When you have finished, share your description with the class.

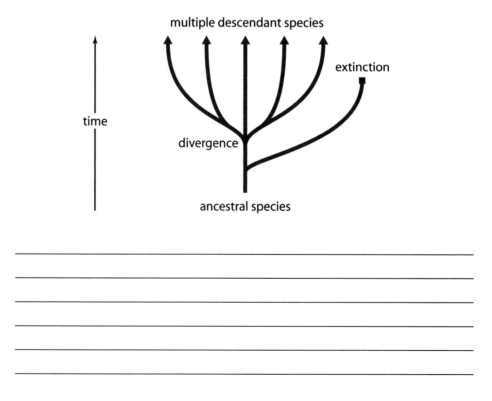

ADAPTIVE RADIATION

_____

_____

_____

_____

_____

_____

ACTIVITY ⑪

Give a Group Presentation

In this speaking activity, you and your group (four students total) will give a presentation on a biology topic. You will explain one feature of a specific animal.

Some Information about Group Presentations

Group presentations are commonly used by teachers in colleges and universities. The benefits are many, from saving time and still allowing everyone to speak to sharing ideas and doing research together.

However, working together on a group project or presentation has its pitfalls as well. One of the biggest complaints about group presentations is the lack of participation by all the members of the group. There is nothing more frustrating than working very hard to contribute to the group's progress only to find that one member of the group did not do his or her work. Most teachers do not take this excuse into consideration when grading an incomplete presentation, and the whole group may get a low grade.

For this reason, it is imperative that each member of the group do the work assigned to him or her. If everyone shares the labor, the final product is more likely to be complete.

Task

In your group, choose an animal to research. Your presentation should concentrate on one particular feature of this animal, for example, a giraffe's long neck or a parrot's curved beak. Each student will be responsible for a section of the presentation:

1. introduction (one student)
2. body or main points (two students)
3. conclusion (one student)

Guidelines

1. Decide on the topic of your presentation.
2. Choose one student to be responsible for each section of the presentation: introduction (1 student), body or main points (2 students), and conclusion (1 student).
3. Create at least one visual for the presentation. This can be a poster, photo, transparency, or something as simple as a graphic you put on the board. Just as in lectures, the more information you provide to your audience, the more they will learn.
4. Limit your presentation to no more than 7 minutes.

Organize the Presentation

While there is more than one way to organize a presentation, you can use the outline below to help you map out your ideas. See Appendix 2 for more information on making oral presentations.

SAMPLE OUTLINE

1. INTRODUCTION:

interesting hook: _____

_____

main topic: _____

2. BODY / main ideas:

Point 1

transition

Point 2

transition

Point 3

3. CONCLUSION:

restate the main points:

give opinion, suggestion, or prediction

Key Concepts 1: Listening, Note Taking, and Speaking Across the Disciplines

Alternative Presentation Topics

The field of biology is vast. Below are some additional topics that you may want to consider for your group presentation.

- a formal definition of biology
- photosynthesis
- how heredity works
- developmental stages of the embryo
- identifying species
- how HIV occurs
- some human uses of plants

ACTIVITY

Use the Internet

On the Internet, search for a timeline of important discoveries in biology. (Try typing *biology timelines* in a search engine.) Choose one or two biological discoveries and share the information with the class. Be prepared to discuss why you think this event is important in the field of biology.

For more activities and information, go to the *Key Concepts 1* website at *elt.heinle.com/keyconcepts.*

PHI 1010
Introduction to Philosophy (3)

This course is an introduction into the human ability to think consciously and critically about existence and experience. This class will cover several basic areas of philosophical thought, including the idea of consciousness and being, the concept of free will, the nature and categories of human knowledge, ethics, logic, the existence of God, and methods of philosophical inquiry.

6 · From the Social Sciences: · Philosophy

Philosophy is a field of inquiry that dates back more than two thousand years. A philosophy major in college explores the basic questions of life: how we relate to the world, and what it means to be a thinking human being. Read the above college catalog description of a philosophy course.

Now find a course description for an introductory philosophy course from your community college or university catalog. What similarities do the two courses have? What are the differences?

This chapter will help you understand some **key concepts** of philosophy, such as

- the origins of philosophy
- the connection between human existence and philosophy
- the differences and similarities among philosophy, religion, and science
- the nature of *existentialism* and how it differs from earlier philosophical thought

You will also practice some academic skills for success.

Get Ready to Listen

ACTIVITY **1**

Brainstorming and Discussion

A big part of philosophy is deciding what is true and what is right and wrong. Here are some questions that philosophers have been asking over the millennia. What do you think? Circle your answers. Then compare and discuss your reasons for them in a small group.

1. Do people have free will (the ability to change their destiny) or is our life's path already decided for us?   FREE WILL   PATH DECIDED

2. If you could live forever, would you want to?   YES   NO

3. Do we have a soul?   YES   NO

4. Is there such a thing as good and evil?   YES   NO

5. Are people basically bad or good?   BAD   GOOD   NEITHER

6. Is there a way for all of the people of the world to live together in peace and happiness?   YES   NO

Listen and Respond

Listen for Phrasal Verbs

With a partner or a small group, listen to the conversations. Each conversation includes a phrasal verb. Circle the letter that contains the best definition of each phrasal verb.

1. What does *bring out* mean?
   a. include
   b. take away from
   c. show clearly
   d. remove

2. What does the student mean by *think over*?
   a. finish
   b. think about more
   c. decide now
   d. think about later

3. What does the woman mean by *find out* about the homework?
   a. share her homework
   b. take her homework out
   c. look for her homework
   d. get information about the homework

4. What does the man mean by *read on*?
   a. read further in the chapter
   b. read the part on basic terms
   c. skip the basic terms section
   d. read the basic terms section after he reads the rest of the chapter

5. What does *open things up* mean?
   a. begin the new chapter
   b. let students talk about what he has said
   c. talk more about the chapter
   d. ask students to look up things for discussion

6. What does *split up* the class mean?
   a. put part of the class in the library
   b. give the class assignments
   c. divide the class into groups
   d. take the class to the library

7. What does the student mean when she says that she *left out* an important point?
   a. The professor lost the student's paper.
   b. The student left her paper in the classroom.
   c. The student left the class without her paper.
   d. The student did not include some important information.

8. What does the student mean when he says he has to *track down* answers?
   a. Go to a track.
   b. Look for information that is difficult to find.
   c. Make a list of questions for Monday.
   d. Keep track of Professor Cole's questions.

Vocabulary

Academic Word List

Practice reading and saying aloud these vocabulary words. How many of the words do you already know?

1. **assume** [ə so͞om´] v. to take for granted; suppose

   Plato <u>assumed</u> that objects in the physical world were imperfect copies of abstract forms and concepts in an invisible world.

2. **category** [kăt´ ĭ gôr´ ē] n. a class or division in a system of classification

   The philosophical <u>category</u> of aesthetics studies concepts of art and beauty.

3. **formula** [fôr´ myə lə] n. a method of doing or treating something that uses a set, accepted model or approach

   Pythagoras was a philosopher and mathematician who devised geometric <u>formulas</u> to explain linear relationships.

4. **normal** [nôr´ məl] adj. standard or typical

   It was <u>normal</u> a few hundred years ago to see science and philosophy as one subject.

5. **percent** [pər sĕnt´] n. one part in a hundred

   Unlike scientists, philosophers cannot be 100 <u>percent</u> sure that they are right.

6. **perceive** [pər sēv´] v. to become aware of (something) through the senses, especially to see or hear; to achieve understanding of

   Empirical philosophers say that the only way to correctly <u>perceive</u> the world is through physical observation.

7. **secure** [sĭ kyo͝or´] adj. free from danger, attack, or loss; free from fear, anxiety, or doubt; firmly fastened; assured, certain. v. to guard something from danger or risk of loss

   Religion gives people a <u>secure</u> feeling. (adj)
   Many people <u>secure</u> themselves against new ways of thinking. (v)

8. **significant** [sĭg nĭf´ ĭ kənt] adj. having a meaning; meaningful

   Hegel was a <u>significant</u> German philosopher.

9. **site** [sīt] n. the place where something is, was, or will be located

   Ancient Athens was the <u>site</u> where Western philosophy began.

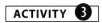 **Vocabulary Practice**

A. Some words from the Academic Word List that you just reviewed are commonly used with some nouns. In each item below, find and underline the two words that you think are most commonly used with the bold vocabulary words or phrases. The first one has been done for you.

1. **a box of:**   <u>cookies</u>   milk   <u>candy</u>

2. (10, 50, etc.) **percent of:**   the population   (your) grade   love

3. **a formula for:**   disaster   feelings   success

4. **a significant:**   number of ...   amount of ...   many of ...

5. **assume:**   the kind   the worst   the best

6. **to feel secure about:**   a job   a relationship   a possibility

7. **to perceive:**   a lesson   the truth   danger

8. **a normal:**   job   day   accident

B. In the spaces provided below, write one sentence for each vocabulary word from Part A.

1. _____

2. _____

3. _____

4. _____

5. _____

6. _____

7. _____

8. _____

C. Check your answers to Part A with a partner. Then connect the word shapes below on the left with the ones on the right; underline the correct *italicized* words in the middle boxes to complete the sentences.

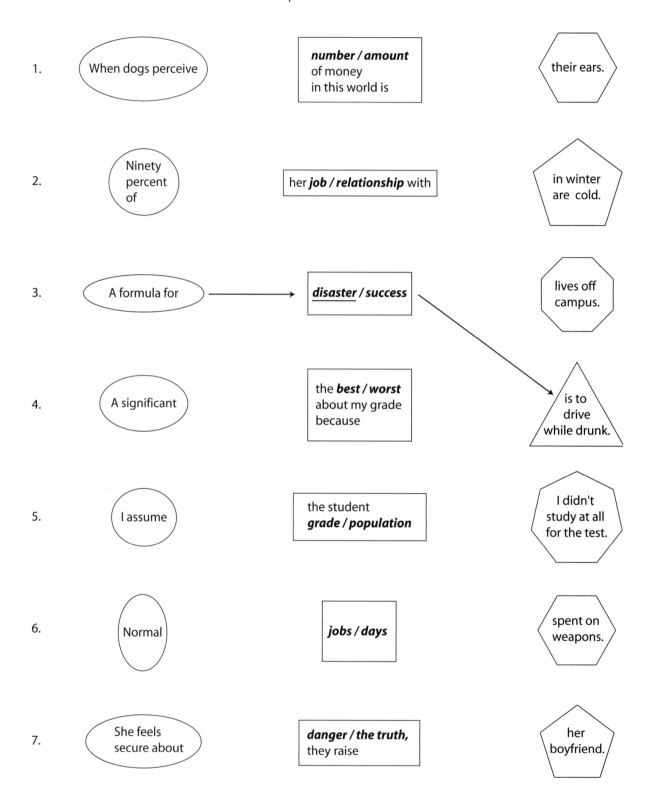

1. When dogs perceive

number / amount of money in this world is

their ears.

2. Ninety percent of

her *job / relationship* with

in winter are cold.

3. A formula for

disaster / *success*

lives off campus.

4. A significant

the *best / worst* about my grade because

is to drive while drunk.

5. I assume

the student *grade / population*

I didn't study at all for the test.

6. Normal

jobs / days

spent on weapons.

7. She feels secure about

danger / the truth, they raise

her boyfriend.

Taking Notes: Paragraph Method

Using Paragraphs in Note Taking

Some students' preferred way of taking notes is to write the information in paragraph form. Writing notes as paragraphs is different from creating your own original paragraph. Paragraphs you write in note taking are shorter, and they don't include every word that the speaker is saying. However, they should include any key words you hear. It is often easier to use paragraphs in note taking if the lecturer is speaking slowly.

Read the following paragraph and look at the example of the paragraph method of note taking that follows it.

> The history of Western philosophy began in ancient Greece around the sixth century B.C., when philosophers first made theories about the basic elements that make up the physical world. In the fifth century B.C., the philosopher Plato developed the idea of the atom—almost 2,000 years before the atom was proved to exist. The fifth century B.C. Greeks also turned their attention to questions about human social reality and the nature of thought. The method of logical inquiry developed by Socrates, Plato's teacher, still exists today in science. This Greek tradition of investigation continued later through much of the Roman Empire. Then with the coming of the medieval period, from around 1100 to 1500, sometimes called the Dark Ages, only the scholars of the Catholic Church kept these ideas alive, though mainly within a religious context. At the end of the Middle Ages, the Renaissance (a French word that means *rebirth*) began the modern age of philosophy, in which the rise of science and humanistic (nonreligious) thought completely challenged the philosophy of both medieval religious scholars and the ancient Greeks. Since that time, the field of philosophy has grown tremendously and is very different from those first thoughts the ancient Greeks had. However, even now we can still see their ideas, formed so many centuries ago, in the concepts of modern philosophical and scientific thought.

Here is an example of the paragraph method of note taking for the paragraph you just read:

West. philosophy began in 6th cen. Greece about elements of physical world. In 5th cen. Plato dev. atom theory, and Socrates dev. logical inquiry about human social reality and nature of thought. In medieval Dark Ages, only Catholic scholars kept these ideas alive. Modern age of philo. began in Renaissance with science and humanistic thought. Philo. has grown and is different in modern times, but we can see ideas formed in earlier centuries.

Listen and Respond

Listen and Use Strategies You Learned

First Listening: Listen and Take Notes As you listen to this mini-lecture from an Introduction to Philosophy class, take notes using the paragraph method. Remember, you do not have to write down all the information you hear.

[blank box for notes]

Second Listening: Listen for Discourse Markers Listen again to the mini-lecture and underline the discourse markers below that you hear. Then match the underlined markers to their meanings.

Today I'll go over …   can be defined as …   a case in point
A type of   If we put it another way   Now,   Moreover,
Nevertheless …   can be divided into …   in terms of   In conclusion,

1. _____ (to finish)

2. _____ (a kind of)

3. _____ (but)

4. _____ (according to)

5. _____ (a good example)

6. _____ (can mean)

Answer Questions about the Mini-Lecture

Use your notes in Activity 4 to help you circle the letter of the answers to the following questions.

1. Which of the following questions would most probably NOT be studied in a philosophy class?
   a. Is there a God?
   b. What is the purpose of life?
   c. Which animals are most like human beings?
   d. Is there a correct way to behave toward other people?

2. Metaphysics does NOT include inquiry about
   a. God.
   b. self.
   c. free will.
   d. formulas.

3. How are science and philosophy similar?
   a. They both ask questions about why we are here.
   b. They are both based on faith.
   c. Empiricism is used in both of them.
   d. They both ask questions about metaphysics.

4. How are science and philosophy different?
   a. Science generally asks "how" questions and philosophy generally asks "why" questions.
   b. Science uses the empirical method.
   c. Only philosophy is based on faith.
   d. Only science is based on faith.

5. Which of the following is a similarity between philosophy and religion?
   a. Faith is important in both of them.
   b. They both are concerned with the meaning of life.
   c. They both use the empirical method.
   d. They both require proof.

6. Which of the following have the least in common?
   a. religion and philosophy
   b. science and philosophy
   c. science and religion
   d. metaphysics and religion

7. Which of the following is concerned with the question "Does God exist?"?
   a. religion and science
   b. science and philosophy
   c. religion
   d. philosophy

Listening Strategy: Understand Reduction Strings

Understand Reduction Strings

Students learning English often say that when Americans speak, they say all the words together very quickly and it's difficult to understand them. In fact, "talking fast" is a common feature of speaking in any language—people shorten (reduce) and put (string) words together to speed up their speech. This creates reduction strings, or word strings. You can learn to listen for standard phrases people use in English that will make understanding word strings a lot easier.

Examples of Word Strings

1. Look at the long groups of letters below. Say them all together. Notice the schwa (ə) symbol you learned about in Chapter 4.

   wədyəwanədu   wenəryəgənəgo   wədjədu   duyəwanəgo

   Although these word strings look confusing, they are all common questions in American English. Can you guess what they are?

2. Try to match the questions below to the letter combinations above.

   When are you going to go?   Do you want to go?
   What do you want to do?   What did you do?

3. Can you read and pronounce these questions?

   What əryəgənədu this weekend? (What are you going to do this weekend?)
   Where aryəgənəgo? (Where are you going to go?)
   Who əryəgənəgo with? (Who are you going to go with?)

Tips for Understanding Word Strings

Look at the capitalized letters at the beginnings and ends of these questions.

   WA-də-yə-wa-nə-DU?   WEN-ər-yə-gənə-GO?
   WA-djə-DU?   DU-yə-wanə-GO?

These first and last syllables are important parts of the word string that can change a question: *what/do, when/go, do/go*. Once you recognize that the center parts of the string mean *do you, are you, did you*, and *you want*, you can concentrate on the first and last parts of the word string to understand many types of questions.

ACTIVITY 6

Listen and Write Sentences

A. You will hear a speaker ask some questions and make some statements. The speaker speaks rapidly and uses word strings. Study the word strings in parentheses below and say them aloud to get a better idea of what the speaker will say. In the blank spaces, write out every word that is spoken in the question, not just what you hear. The numbers in parentheses tell you how many words are in the sentences.

1. (... yəgənə ...) (7) _____
   _____ ?

2. (... duyə ...) (6) _____
   _____ ?

3. (... lyə ...) (6) _____
   _____ ?

4. (... canchə ...) (7) _____
   _____ ?

5. (... yə ...) (6) _____
   _____ ?

6. (... izee ...) (8) _____
   _____ ?

7. (... dəzee ...) (5) _____
   _____ ?

8. (... dono ...) (5) _____
   _____ .

9. (... cudn ...) (6) _____
   _____ .

10. (... wudn ...) (7) _____
   _____ .

B. Below are the responses to the questions you wrote in Part A, but they're not in order. Cover your questions in Part A with a piece of paper and listen to the tape again. Number the responses below as they answer the questions and statements on the tape. The first one has been done for you.

_____ Let me help you.

_____ No, she isn't here today.

_____ By bus.

_**1**_ Kathy and John

_____ In about an hour

_____ The last bus to my house leaves in a few minutes.

_____ That's too bad.

_____ Why? Is she sick?

_____ Yes, I did it right after class.

_____ Yes, he bought it this morning.

Vocabulary

Academic Word List

Practice reading and saying aloud these vocabulary words. How many of the words do you already know?

1. **appropriate** [ə prō′ prē ĭt] adj. suitable for a particular person, occasion, or place; proper

   Philosophers believe that the <u>appropriate</u> way to live is to question and examine things.

2. **community** [kə myōō′ nĭ tē] n. a group of people living in the same city or district and under the same government; a group of people who have close ties, as through common ties or interests

   Socrates was forced to kill himself because his ideas and actions upset powerful members of his <u>community</u>.

3. **complex** [kəm plĕks′] *or* [kŏm′ plĕks′] adj. consisting of many important parts or factors; difficult to understand or explain

   Advanced Logic is a very <u>complex</u> subject.

4. **consequence** [kŏn′ sĭ kwĕns′] n. something that follows from an action or condition; a result

   The German philosopher Marx believed that a classless society would be a <u>consequence</u> of a Communist revolution.

5. **constitute** [kŏn′ stĭ tōōt′] v. to be the elements or parts of something; compose; to set up, establish

   Aristotle believed that there were four elements that <u>constituted</u> the nature and direction of reality and experience.

6. **culture** [kŭl′ chər] n. the arts, beliefs, customs, institutions, and all other products of human work at a particular time

   The German academic <u>culture</u> has produced great philosophical works.

7. **issue** [ĭsh′ ōō] n. a subject being discussed; a question under debate. v. to come out; to flow out

   Free will is a philosophical <u>issue</u> that has been discussed for thousands of years. (n)
   The Danish philosopher Kierkegaard <u>issued</u> writings considered to be existential. (v)

8. **potential** [pə tĕn′ shəl] adj. possible. n. capacity for growth, development, or coming into existence

   Humanists believe that human beings have the <u>potential</u> for both good and evil. (n)
   One of the <u>potential</u> risks of studying too much philosophy is losing touch with current events. (adj)

9. **reside** [rĭ zīd′] v. to live in a place permanently

   The French philosopher Descartes traveled much of Europe, but in his later years he <u>resided</u> in Holland.

10. **similar** [sĭm′ ə lər] adj. related in appearance or nature; alike but not exactly the same

    The ancient Greek Stoic philosophers and Buddhists have <u>similar</u> ideas about accepting the troubles of life.

11. **tradition** [trə dĭsh′ ən] n. the passing down of beliefs and customs from generation to generation

    Philosophical inquiry is a <u>tradition</u> that has continued over many centuries.

Vocabulary Practice

These vocabulary words are used for more than talking about philosophy. Look at the *italicized* explanations in parentheses in the following sentences. Susan was explaining things to her teacher, and she put her ideas in parentheses because she couldn't think of the right words. What are some more accurate (and shorter) words to say what she means? Replace the underlined words with one of the vocabulary words you just studied.

1. The celebration of Thanksgiving is an American (*You know, it's* a long-time repeated thing that a group of people does together) _tradition_____.

2. Gun control is an (*Let's see, the word I'm trying to think of means* a subject that a lot of people talk and disagree about.) _____ in America.

3. My sister has the (*I think it's like* a natural ability that she can develop.) _____ to be a great singer.

4. There is a large Arab-American (*What word means* a group of people who live in the same area?) _____ in Michigan.

5. These instructions are very (*difficult to understand because of all of the different parts*) _____. I can't figure them out!

6. I fell from a tree when I was a child and as a (*It's like, now,* as a result of my accident) _____ I'm afraid of high places.

7. I can't really think of the (*another word that means* right) _____ words to describe him to you.

8. My sister and I have a (*um,* she looks like me) _____ appearance.

9. A lot of people in my part of the country (*Do you know another word for* live in an area?) _____ in small towns.

10. My grandparents don't like the (*uh, you know,* the music, styles, attitudes, ideas) _____ of young people today.

Use Discourse Markers

The discourse markers underlined in the sentences below are the ones you did not use from Activity 4. You will hear them in the next lecture. Their meanings are in the box. Write the meanings in the appropriate sentences below.

~~Today I'll talk about~~	and also	at this time
separated	one more	basically
say the same thing in different words		

1. <u>Today I'll go over</u> the material in Lesson 2.

   Today I'll talk about

2. <u>Another</u> thing I like to do is read French philosophers.

   _____

3. Sports can be <u>divided into</u> two categories: one-on-one and team competitions.

   _____

4. I like the Japanese proverb "Even monkeys fall from trees." Or, if we <u>put it another way</u>, "Nobody is perfect."

   _____

5. I'm staying home. I'm tired. <u>Moreover</u>, I have a headache.

   _____

6. <u>Fundamentally</u>, all human beings want to be happy.

   _____

7. <u>Now</u>, let's go over what will be on the test.

   _____

Listen and Respond

Listen and Use Strategies You Learned

First Listening: Listen for Vocabulary Words You will hear the extended lecture two times. The first time, listen for the vocabulary words in the box below. Write them between the words that come before and after them in the lecture.

potential	issue	constitutes	community
similar	consequences	appropriate	culture
resided	complex	~~traditions~~	standard

1. all systems and __*traditions*__ in society

2. about what _____ existentialism

3. of whom _____ in Western Europe

4. existentialist _____ *does* agree

5. our _____ as human beings

6. important _____ to Nietzsche

7. arguments are _____, but,

8. but not _____ religious faith

9. seem _____ for

10. actions and the _____ of these actions

11. very _____ to the ideas

12. artistic _____ they created

Second Listening: Listen and Take Notes Now listen to the extended lecture on existentialism again and take notes on the following page. Use any of the note-taking methods you have learned in this book:

- outlining, Chapter 2, pages 26–27;
- word maps, Chapter 3, pages 44–45;
- the Cornell method, Chapter 4, pages 67–68;
- key words, Chapter 5, page 91, or
- the paragraph method in this chapter, page 111

ACTIVITY 10

Answer Questions about the Extended Lecture

Use your notes from the lecture you just heard and circle the letter of the answer to the following questions.

1. All existentialists believe that
   a. the individual can't believe anything.
   b. the individual must question everything.
   c. all systems in society are wrong.
   d. all religious faith is wrong.

2. All existentialists believe that
   a. being responsible for one's actions is more important than finding the truth
   b. being responsible for one's actions is less important than finding the truth
   c. an individual's actions are always a consequence of what he or she truly believes
   d. finding truth and being responsible for one's actions are equally important

3. Nietzsche said that
   a. Christianity was basically wrong but had some good ideas.
   b. The human race will not survive if people don't change the way they think.
   c. The "Overman" would be a new kind of religious person.
   d. Christianity was not the primary reason for all the world's problems.

4. Nietzsche and Kierkegaard disagree about
   a. standard religious faith
   b. the individual's need to question traditional ideas
   c. the importance of faith
   d. the responsibility of the individual to find meaning in life

5. Sartre's beliefs about religious faith
   a. were similar to Kierkegaard's beliefs
   b. were similar to those of most existentialists
   c. were completely different from Nietzsche's
   d. did not address the important questions about life

6. Sartre thought that
   a. God exists but does not give life meaning
   b. only a belief in God can give meaning to one's life
   c. the starting point is to believe in God
   d. life can have meaning without a belief in God

7. Which of these existentialist thinkers might agree with the following statement: *A person's soul may continue after that person dies.*
   a. Sartre
   b. Nietzsche
   c. Kierkegaard
   d. all of the above

8. From what you have heard, which subject below do you think would be of least interest to most existentialists?
   a. chemistry
   b. politics
   c. literature
   d. art

Think Critically

Use your notes on the extended lecture to decide how an existentialist would feel about the following questions. Circle *yes* or *no* for each statement. Your teacher may call on you to explain your choices.

1. People should do anything that they want to do.   YES   NO
2. Some basic things in life are right and wrong for all people.   YES   NO
3. Morality must be decided by the individual.   YES   NO
4. People are basically bad or good.   YES   NO
5. There is only one truth.   YES   NO
6. The unexamined life is not worth living.   YES   NO
7. People might have souls.   YES   NO
8. Life is meaningless.   YES   NO
9. People should continue to believe they are right,
    even if everyone says they are wrong.   YES   NO
10. If God exists then existentialism is wrong.   YES   NO

SPEAKING ● **Summarizing**

ACTIVITY **12**   *Research and Summarize Topics*

Task

Choose a philosophy topic and give a six- to ten-minute oral summary of it for the class. Remember that philosophy can be a difficult subject, so don't worry about trying to understand or explain a kind of philosophy completely. Just give the main idea and a summary of its important points.

Guidelines

Do the following on your own, with a partner, or with a small group:

1. Read the list of topics in the box below and choose one that interests you. If necessary look the topics up in a dictionary or encyclopedia to find out what they mean.
2. Research your topic in the library or on the Internet.
3. Include these general points in your presentation:
    • fundamental ideas embodied in the philosophy
    • who started it
    • brief history, including important people and what they said
    • your opinion of the ideas in the philosophy
    • a visual—a poster, pictures, diagrams, drawings—to enhance your presentation

    You might even want to use music if it's appropriate for your topic.

4. Avoid reading from notes or a paper; instead, convey the summary of the philosophy in your own words as much as possible.

5. If you are working with a partner or in a small group, make sure each person has an equal part in the presentation.

List of Topics

Free Will	Socratic Method	Epicurianism
The Social Contract	Epistemology	Determinism
Empiricism	Existentialism	Utopianism
Phenomenology	Materialism	Rationalism
Logic	Cynicism	Aesthetics
Dualism	Stoicism	
Ethics	Neoplatonism	

 ACTIVITY **_Find Out about More Key Concepts_**

Find a philosophy instructor or a student who is currently studying philosophy. Question this person about what he or she considers a **key concept** in the field of philosophy. Take notes and share your findings with the class.

For more activities and information, go to the *Key Concepts 1* website at *elt.heinle.com/keyconcepts*.

APPENDIX 1 | Academic Word List Vocabulary[1]

Academic Word List word	Standard American Heritage phonetic spelling
achieve	ə **chēv´**
acquire	ə **kwīr´**
administrate	ăd **mĭn´** ĭ strāt´
affect	ə **fĕkt´**
analyze	**ăn´** ə līz´
approach	ə **prōch´**
appropriate	ə **prō´** prē ĭt
area	**âr´** ē ə
aspect	**ăs´** pĕkt
assess	ə **sĕs´**
assist	ə **sĭst´**
assume	ə **sōōm´**
authority	ə **thôr´** ĭ tē *or* ə **thŏr´** ĭ tē
available	ə **vā´** lə bəl
benefit	**bĕn´** ə fĭt
category	**kăt´** ĭ gôr´ ē
chapter	**chăp´** tər
commission	kə **mĭsh´** ən
community	kə **myōō´** nĭ tē
complex	kəm **plĕks´** *or* **kŏm´** plĕks´
compute	kəm **pyōōt´**
concept	**kŏn´** sĕpt´
conclude	kən **klōōd´**
conduct	kən **dŭkt´** *or* **kŏn´** dŭkt´
consequence	**kŏn´** sĭ kwĕns´
consist (of)	kən **sĭst´**
constitute	**kŏn´** stĭ tōōt´

[1]Coxhead, Averil (2000)

construct	kən strŭkt´
consume	kən sōōm´
context	kŏn´ tĕkst
contract	kŏn´ trăkt´ *or* kən trăkt´
create	krē āt´
credit	krĕd´ ĭt
culture	kŭl´ chər
data	dā´ tə *or* dăt´ ə
define	dĭ fīn´
derive	dĭ rīv´
design	dĭ zīn´
distinct	dĭ stĭngkt´
distribute	dĭ strĭb´ yōōt
economy	ĭ kon´ ə mē
element	ĕl´ ə mənt
environment	ĕn vī´ rən mənt *or* ĕn vī´ ərn mənt
equate	ĭ kwāt´
establish	ĭ stăb´ lĭsh
estimate	ĕs´ tə māt *or* ĕs´ tə mĭt
evaluate	ĭ văl´ yōō āt´
evident	ĕv´ ĭ dənt
export	ĭk spôrt´ *or* ĕk´ spôrt´
factor	făk´ tər
feature	fē´ chər
final	fī´ nəl
finance	fə năns´ *or* fī´ năns´
focus	fō´ kəs
formula	fôr´ myə lə
function	fŭngk´ shən
identify	ī dĕn´ tə fī
impact	ĭm´ păkt´
income	ĭn´ kŭm
indicate	ĭn´ dĭ kāt´

individual	ĭn´ də vĭj´ o̅o̅ əl
injure	ĭn´ jər
institute	ĭn´ stĭ too̅t
interpret	ĭn tûr´ prĭt
invest	ĭn vĕst´
involve	ĭn vŏlv´
issue	ĭsh´ oo̅
item	ī´ təm
journal	jûr´ nəl
labor	lā´ bər
legal	lē´ gəl
legislate	lĕj´ ĭ slāt´
maintain	mān tān´
major	mā´ jər
method	mĕth´ əd
normal	nôr´ məl
obtain	əb tān´
occur	ə kûr´
participate	pär tĭs´ ə pāt´
perceive	pər sēv´
percent	pər sĕnt´
period	pĭr´ ē əd
policy	pŏl´ ĭ sē
positive	pŏz´ ĭ tĭv
potential	pə tĕn´ shəl
previous	pre´ vē əs
primary	prī´ mĕr´ ē *or* prī´ mə rē
principle	prĭn´ sə pəl
proceed	prə cēd´
process	prŏs´ ĕs´
purchase	pûr´ chĭs
range	rānj
region	rē´ jən

regulate	**rĕg´** yə lāt´
relevant	**rĕl´** ə vənt
require	rĭ **kwīr´**
research	rĭ **sûrch´** *or* **rē´** sûrch
reside	rĭ **zīd´**
resource	**rē´** sôrs´ *or* rĭ **sôrs´**
respond	rĭ **spŏnd´**
restrict	rĭ **strĭkt´**
role	rōl
section	**sĕk´** shən
sector	**sĕk´** tər *or* **sĕk´** tôr´
secure	sĭ **kyŏŏr´**
seek	sēk
select	sĭ **lĕkt´**
significant	sĭg **nĭf´** ĭ kənt
similar	**sĭm´** ə lər
site	sīt
source	sôrs
specific	spĭ **sĭf´** ĭk
strategy	**străt´** ə jē
structure	**strŭk´** chər
survey	**sûr´** vā *or* sər **vā´**
text	tĕkst
theory	**thē´** ə rē *or* **thîr´** ē
tradition	trə **dĭsh´** ən
transfer	trăns **fûr´** *or* **trăns´** fər
vary	**vâr´** ē *or* **văr´** ē

Speaking in Class: Strategies for Presentations and Interactive Communication

Developing Confidence

Imagination Exercise

- Picture yourself in front of an audience.
- Watch yourself stepping out in front of the audience with confidence.
- Listen to the silence fall upon the room as you begin to speak.
- Feel the attention of the audience as you drive home point after point with confidence.
- Feel the warmth of the applause as you leave the platform.
- Hear the words of appreciation after your speech is over.

Helpful Tips

Seize every opportunity to practice speaking!

- Ask questions in class.
- Say hello to someone new every day.
- Join a club or an organization.

Develop confidence!

- Remember that you are not alone in your fear; more than 90 percent of the university population is afraid to speak in public.
- Some **stage fright** is useful! Adrenaline can make you think faster, speak more fluently and with greater intensity than normal.
- The *main cause* of your fear of public speaking is simply that you are not used to speaking in public!

Organizing Your Presentation

The Introduction

The introduction should contain a **hook** and the **main topic** that will be discussed (in that order).

The Hook

Fishermen use hooks to catch fish, and speakers use hooks to capture an audience. A hook should be an interesting

- quote
- statistic
- question
- anecdote (brief story)
- shared experience
- timeless truth

that is connected to your topic.

Example of a Hook

In a personal speech about a grandfather, the speaker uses this hook:

> "It was 1912, the same year that the Titanic sailed. But instead of traveling from England to New York, he went from Naples to Boston. The ship was crowded and dirty. Yet he survived the trip and countless other disasters. He was a man of great dignity. He was my grandfather."

Notice how the speaker did not begin the speech with, "Today I'm going to tell you about my grandfather." The audience is drawn in—hooked—by this little story of someone traveling on a ship to the United States. The speaker lets the audience know the main topic of the speech in the last sentence of the introduction: "He was my grandfather."

The Body

The body of a speech should be organized into main points with specific examples or supporting information. The audience should be able to pick out discourse markers and transitions to note shifts in the speech.

The Conclusion

The conclusion of an informational speech should contain two things:

1. a restatement or summary sentence
2. something that will leave your audience thinking about what you said

Here are a few examples of conclusions:

- a suggestion
- an opinion
- a prediction

Interactive Speaking: Asking and Answering Questions

When we listen to someone lecture, we sometimes want to ask questions to clarify a point or to get additional information. If someone is speaking and you want more information on the topic, there are good ways and bad ways to signal what you want. A bad way is to simply ask a question briskly: *What? Huh? What did you say? I didn't get that.*

Not only are these questions nonspecific, but to many people they sound rude. A better way to ask for additional or repeated information is to restate a part of what the speaker was talking about and then introduce your question. This method gives the speaker a frame of reference and invites a more relevant answer.

For example, note the differences between two types of questions. A speaker has just finished giving a presentation on the benefits of community colleges. A member of the audience asks: "John, where did you get your statistics?" While the information in the question is clear, the speaker might not know which statistics the audience member is referring to. A better way of phrasing the question is: "John, you just said something about the cost of community college studies. **My question is** … where did you get the statistics?"

When you give the speaker a frame of reference and signal that a question is going to come (in this case, *my question is* …), the speaker will listen more carefully to the question and be able to give a more specific answer.

APPENDIX 3

Sample Evaluation Forms (Gradesheets) for Oral Presentations

I. Individual Presentations

Name of Speaker: _____

Speech Topic: _____

Date: _____

Content

Introduction

Creativity	6	5	4	3	2	1
Relevance to main topic	6	5	4	3	2	1

Transitions

Presence/use of transitions	6	5	4	3	2	1

Body

Organization of ideas / details	6	5	4	3	2	1

Conclusion

Summary of main areas	6	5	4	3	2	1

Content Score: _____ (max. 30 points)

Delivery

Eye Contact	6	5	4	3	2	1
Confidence	6	5	4	3	2	1

Voice

Volume	6	5	4	3	2	1
Speed	6	5	4	3	2	1
Intonation	6	5	4	3	2	1

Delivery Score: _____ (max. 30 points)

Total Score: _____ (max. 60 points)

Comments:

II. Group Presentations

What Will Be Evaluated

Group Grade	Individual Grade
Information	Pronunciation
Completion	Clarity
Organization	Fluency
Presentation	Presence

Note: Group presentations will be timed.

Maximum time: _____ minutes per speaker
Going over the maximum time limit will result in a lower grade!

Names of Speakers: _____

_____

_____

_____

_____

Speech Topic: _____

Date: _____

Group Evaluation

Information / content	6	5	4	3	2	1
Completion	6	5	4	3	2	1
Organization	6	5	4	3	2	1
Presentation / delivery	6	5	4	3	2	1

Group Score: _____ (max. 24 points)

Individual Evaluation

Pronunciation	6	5	4	3	2	1
Clarity	6	5	4	3	2	1
Fluency (grammar / vocabulary accuracy)	6	5	4	3	2	1
Presence / delivery	6	5	4	3	2	1

Individual Score: _____ (max. 24 points)

Total Score: _____ (max. 48 points)

Comments:

III. Sample Student Feedback Forms

Basic Form

Basic Listening Task

Name of Speaker: _____

Date: _____

1. What is the main topic of the speech? _____

2. What was the purpose of the speech? _____

_____

3. Write one specific detail from the speech. _____

_____

Detailed Form

Speech Evaluation Form

Name of Speaker: _____

Speech Topic: _____

Date: _____

Content/Organization:

1. What was the hook or introduction of the presentation?

   question   anecdote   statistic   quotation   Other: _____

2. What was the main point of the presentation? _____

_____

3. How did the presentation end?   *summary   suggestion   opinion   prediction*

Nonverbal Communication:
(Circle one)

4. Eye contact: excellent   very good   fair   needs work

5. Hand / body gestures: excellent   very good   fair   needs work

Verbal Communication:
(Circle one)

6. Pronunciation: excellent   very good   fair   needs work

7. Speed: excellent   very good   fair   needs work

Notes: _____

_____

_____

APPENDIX 4 | Note-Taking Symbols

Many students like to use note-taking symbols during lectures. These types of symbols can save valuable time because they replace entire words or phrases with a shortened representation. However, because there is no one universal symbol for a particular word or phrase, symbols can be confusing.

You should not feel obligated to use symbols if you feel uncomfortable with them. If you are not used to the symbols or their verbal representations, you may make mistakes and use the wrong symbols. Symbols should always be used in the same way—use them only if you feel comfortable with them and know them well. If you need to spend a few seconds during a lecture trying to remember the symbol for something, you are defeating the purpose of saving time.

Common Note-Taking Symbols

Symbol	Meaning	Example
=	equals; is	Martin Luther King = activist
<	less than	The population of the US is < 300 million.
>	more than	The average state income is > $25,000.
&	and	Smith & Jones developed the new formula.
w/	with	Biologists work w/ the scientific method.
↑	increase	If the war continues, military spending will ↑.
↓	decrease	Profits will ↓ at Microsoft this year.
e.g.,	for example (Latin *exempli gratia*)	The troops needed supplies, e.g., weapons, vehicles, and more food rations.
i.e.,	that is; as in (Latin *id est*)	The leader was eliminated; i.e., he was assassinated.
≅	approximately	The temperature is ≅ 76 degrees.
∴	therefore	Business is going well. ∴ stockholders will get better dividends.
→	causes	Smoking → cancer.
#	number	The # of AIDS cases is rising.
aka	also known as	The plague, aka the "Black Death," spread throughout Europe.
w/o	without	He was arrested w/o warning.
%	percent	The % of homeless is alarming
~	between	The current rate of inflation is ~ 1% and 2%.

Other Guidelines for Note Taking

1. Shorten dates: (July 4, 1776 = 7/4/1776).

2. Use the first syllable and/or first few letters of the second syllable (history = hist).

3. Omit vowels (develop = dvlp).

4. Omit prepositions and articles (the Chancellor of Germany = Chancellor Germany).

5. After the first use, abbreviate proper nouns (Scholastic Aptitude Test = SAT).

Note-Taking Strategies

Step 1: Observe

Bring all the materials you need.

Sit front and center.

Review the information from the previous lesson before class begins.

Notice your writing.

Postpone debate.

Don't judge lecture styles.

Participate in class activities.

Listen for repetition.

Listen for discourse markers.

Watch the blackboard/overhead.

Notice the interest level of the instructor.

Step 2: Record

Use the Cornell method of note taking.

Use mind maps.

Write notes in outline form.

Write notes in paragraph form.

Use key words.

Use diagrams.

Copy information from the board.

Use only one side of the paper.

Use note cards.

Separate your thoughts from the instructor's thoughts.

Label, number, and date all your notes.

Use abbreviations.

Leave blank space in your notes.

Use a tape recorder.

Step 3: Review

Review notes within 24 hours.

Edit your notes.

Fill in key words in the left-hand column.

Use key words as study guides.

NOTE: If possible, type your notes. If you can't type them, write them clearly and neatly so you'll be able to read them later.

Discourse Markers[2]

The discourse markers are listed by function.

Introducing

In my talk today,
Today, we're going to discuss
The purpose of this talk is

My topic today is
Today, I'll go over
Today we are going to consider

Giving Background Information

It is clear
It is understood
As we have all read

It goes without saying
As we know

Defining

X can be defined as
X is known as

X is a type of Y which
X is actually

Listing

First,
Second,
The next point I'd like to cover is
Another

To begin with,
Next,
Finally,

Showing a Connection

pertaining to

in connection with

Giving Examples

For example,
X is a case in point.
Take X, for example.
Let me give you some
  specific examples:

For instance,
Take X, for instance.
The following are
  some common examples:

[2]Adapted from "Listening Comprehension and Note Taking." UEFAP. 9 Dec. 2002. *http://www.uefap.co.uk/listen/struct/liststru.htm*.

Emphasizing

The crucial point is
We should bear in mind that
I want to stress
What's more,
This goes to show that

I'd like to emphasize
Fundamentally,
Furthermore
It follows, then
In effect,

Clarifying

In other words,
Basically,
i.e.,
Let me put it another way.

That is to say,
If we put it another way,
What I mean to say is

Shifting Subtopics

Now
OK
Now, I'd like to turn to
Moving on,

All right
Let's now look at
The next point I'd like to focus on

Giving Further Information

In addition,
Another point
Not only …, but …
as well

Furthermore,
Moreover,
also

Giving Contrasting Information

Although
On the other hand,
Despite

However,
Whereas
Nevertheless,

Classifying

There are X types /
   categories / varieties.

X can be divided into

Setting Parameters

In terms of

In the scope of

Digressing

By the way,
Incidentally,

Before I forget,

Concluding

We've seen that
In short,
Any questions?

In conclusion, I'd like to
To sum up,

NOTE: Words in bold appear in the chapters.

ask out: ask someone to go on a date

be up to: busy with

bring out: reveal or show; make easier to see or experience; produce

bring up: rear (raise) children; mention or introduce a topic

call back: return a telephone call

call off: cancel

call on: ask to speak in class; visit

catch up with: reach the same position or level

check in, check into: register at a hotel

check into: investigate

check out: take a book from the library; investigate

cheer up: make someone feel happier

clean up: make clean and orderly

come across: meet by chance

cross out: draw a line through

cut out: stop an annoying activity

do over: do again

drop by: visit informally; leave something

drop off: leave something/someone at a place

drop out (of): stop going to school, to a class, to a club, etc.

figure out: find the answer by reasoning

fill out: complete a questionnaire or form by writing in the appropriate
   information

fill up: make something completely full or occupied

find out: discover information

get along (with): exist satisfactorily

get back (from): return from a place; receive again

get over: recover from an illness or a bad experience

get through: finish

get up: arise from bed, a chair

give back: return an item to someone

give up: stop trying

go over: review or check carefully

hand in: submit an assignment

hang up: conclude a phone conversation; put clothes on a hanger or a hook

hold off: wait or delay

keep out (of): not enter

keep up (with): stay at the same position or level

kick out (of): force someone to leave

leave out: omit; exclude

look after: take care of

look into: investigate

look out (for): be careful

look over: review or check carefully

look up: look for information in a reference book

make up: compose or form; invent; compensate for something

name after, name for: give a baby the name of someone else

nod off: fall asleep unintentionally

open up: initiate something; begin

pass away: die

pass out: distribute; lose consciousness

pick out: select

pick up: go to get someone; take in one's hand; learn

point out: call attention to

put away: move to a proper place

put back: return to original place

put off: postpone

put out: extinguish a cigarette or cigar

put up with: tolerate

read on: continue reading

run into, run across: meet by chance

run out (of): finish a supply of something

show up: appear, come

shut off: stop a machine, light, faucet, etc.

sit out: not participate or take part in something

split up: separate

take after: resemble

take over: take control

take up: begin a new activity or topic

tear down: demolish; reduce to nothing

tear up: tear into many little pieces

think over: consider carefully

throw away, throw out: discard; get rid of

track down: find

try on: put on clothing to see if it fits

turn down: decrease volume or intensity

turn in: submit an assignment; go to bed

turn off: stop the operation, activity, or flow of something

turn on: cause to begin operation or activity

turn out: arrive or assemble; result; extinguish a light

turn up: increase volume or intensity; find something that was missing

work out: succeed